If He's Not Your Soulmate
He's Just Another John

Anita Dial

authorHOUSE®

AuthorHouse™
1663 Liberty Drive
Bloomington, IN 47403
www.authorhouse.com
Phone: 1 (800) 839-8640

Published by AuthorHouse 01/06/2020

ISBN: 978-1-7283-4151-4 (sc)
ISBN: 978-1-7283-4152-1 (hc)
ISBN: 978-1-7283-4150-7 (e)

Print information available on the last page.

Dedication

This book is dedicated to anyone that believes in Fairy Tales. They do come true, but we forget that in every Fairy Tale there is a villian. This book is dedicated to the one whose life didn't have the happy Fairy Tale ending, because their tale ended with the villian. This book is full of ups and downs, trials and tests, hopes, dreams, wishes and prayers, all a part of lifes' journey. I dedicate this book to the Romantic, the one who believes in love no matter what.

Acknowledgments

I give all praises to God for giving me the ability, the thoughts and the guidance for putting this book together.

Prologue

I was 17 when we met. We were at a club, and he asked me to dance. The DJ was playing a slow jam. He put his arms around me and pulled me in close. It felt so good being in his arms. As we started to dance he whispered in my ear, "I feel you tensing up, just relax and follow me." I said, "ok." He danced me all around the dance floor and it felt like we were floating. At that moment I felt like we were the only two people in the whole club. I could sense his every move and I followed him step for step. We danced like we had been dancing together for years. He had the best slow dance I had ever seen. When the song ended he was very slow about letting me go. Another song started and we started dancing again. I felt I had his full attention and there was no other woman in the place but me. When I got back to my table my girlfriends asked me if I knew that guy. All I could say was "Wow, that was great. I don't know him but I feel like I've known him all my life." I liked the way he danced and it felt good in his arms. I danced with other guys, but I could not stop thinking about the dance with him. I found myself looking for him everytime a song came on. Whenever I looked around the club to see if I could see him, he was looking at me too. We danced again and this time he introduced himself. His name was Jerome Adams. I told him my name and after we danced he asked for my telephone number. I gave it to him. From that moment on until the club closed he stayed near my table watching me as I danced with other guys. I don't remember seeing him dance with any one else. I could not stop looking at him either. Each time our eyes met we smiled at each other. There was something about him that excited me. He was not the first guy that I had met at the club. I had been there before and met other guys, but they did not affect me the way he did. I asked myself what was it about him. I closed my eyes to think, and then I answered my own question. It was the way he approached me when he walked over to my table where I was sitting with four other women and he asked me to dance. It was the way he made me feel when he held me in his arms and pulled me close. It was the way his voice made me relax when he whispered in my ear. It was the way he held onto me after the song had ended. It was the way he looked at me when we exchanged glances across the room. I got a really good feeling just near him. I knew that night he was the man I wanted to be with. But my plan was to go to the club just to dance and have a good time. I wasn't trying to meet anyone other than just someone to dance with. But Jerome got my attention and my heart that night. I was young and I didn't realize what really happened. That night, I met my soulmate. It is amazing how God works. He has a plan for your life, and He knows if you are ready to accept His plan. God allows you to go thru so many things and then He brings you back to where He wanted you to be in the first place. I wasn't ready at age 17 to really appreciate what God had given me. God had to get me ready. I sit back and think about all the things that I've been thru. God has been so good to me. I've had many challenges and many battles. I've had my share of ups and downs. Life has taught me many lessons that I will never forget. I know God loves me because He brought me thru it all, and I am a better person because of Him. I know that God brought our paths back together as only He could and when He felt we were ready. There was still a lesson to learn. I appreciate what God has done. It was a long and eventful journey getting to this place in my life. My journey is the story. Let me take you thru it.

Chapter 1

My journey began the night my sister invited me to go out with her and her friends. I said, "Don't you have to be 18 to go to the club." She said I could pass for 18. All I had to do was just watch her and do what she did and they may not ask me for any ID. I said I would love to go and I hope I got in. I just wanted to go and have a good time, because I loved to dance. I got dressed and my sister picked up her friends and we headed to the club. I was worried that if I couldn't get in my sister would have to take me back home. I didn't want to spoil their fun. When we got to the club there was a guy at the door letting people in. I got nervous. My sister went in first, then one of her friends went in next. I took a deep breath and strutted up to the door like I owned the place. The guy at the door looked me up and down and smiled at me and said, "have a good time." I smiled back and said, "I sure will." When I got inside we sat at a table near the dance floor. I was excited. The waitress came over to our table to get our drink orders. I didn't know what to order, I had never had a drink before. My sister told me to order something mild. She suggested I order a Champale and ask the waitress to add Grenadine to make it taste sweet. The club started filling up and the music was rocking. As I was looking around a guy came over to our table and asked me to dance. I was a little nervous, but once I hit the dance floor I felt better. The first dance was the scariest. The song ended and I was leaving the dance floor when I felt someone grab my hand and ask me to dance. It was a different guy. I danced all night. I had a ball. The one drink that I ordered lasted the whole night because I hardly sat down. I discovered that night that I liked going to the club. We were going out every weekend, so I asked if it would be alright if I brought one of my friends. My sister said it would be alright. It was now five of us going out together. The name of the club was The Batchelor Two. I had no idea what was in store for me, all I knew was I was having a good time dancing and meeting people. I remember that every weekend I would get a blister on my fingers and that was from dancing so much and snapping my fingers so hard. I didn't care I just loved to dance. At the end of the weekend I would start planning what I was going to wear the next weekend. All week long I would rehearse my dance steps. During school me and my girlfriend would meet at our lockers and talk about the good time we had at the club. In our minds we were living a double life. We were high school girls during the week, but on the weekends we were party girls. We would be talking about all the guys we met and when one of our classmates would walk up to us we would change our conversation. We felt like we had a huge secret that no one else knew about. I'm sure we were not the only under age girls going to the clubs, but we didn't care. We started planning the false names we would give to guys that we did not want to talk to and the fake phone numbers we would give out. We even decided we would try ordering a real drink. We wanted to fully enjoy the experience of going to the club.

Chapter 2

I didn't know it but my life was about to change. I met John #1 at the club. He was an older guy. Everyone I met was older because I was only 17. John #1 saw me and he wanted to ask me to dance, but I was sitting with a group of women and he didn't want to ask me to dance in front of all of my friends in case I said no. So he asked his friends to ask my friends to dance so I would be at the table all alone. After everyone was on the dance floor he came over and asked me to dance. I said yes. We danced for a couple of songs. When I went back to my table he found the courage to talk to me. He introduced himself and we just had a nice conversation. He asked my name and my Zodiac Sign. It was 1974, everyone was into the Zodiac Signs. He told me a little about himself and I told him a little about me, but not my age. I did not look 17 so I let him think I was older. Before the club closed he asked for my telephone number. He seemed like a nice guy and I enjoyed talking to him, so I gave him my real telephone number. He called me the next day. We talked for almost an hour and he asked when could he come over. I let him come over the next day. It was a nice summer day, so he took me downtown on the waterfront to see the fireworks. We walked around holding hands and laughing and talking. I enjoyed the fireworks. He was such a gentleman. I was impressed. I remember the first time he took me to his house. He lived with his father. When his father met me I heard his father tell him I was too young for him. I don't know how he knew, but he was right. He was 20. John #1 took me outside and asked me how old I was. When I said 17, he just smiled and he told me he thought I was his age. He said it was not a problem with him if it was not a problem with me. I said it was no problem. I continued to see him for the next several weeks. We didn't really do anything other than him coming to see me, or him taking me over to his house. We went to the drive in movie once. In those several weeks he tried his best to get me to have sex with him. I was still a virgin and I was not ready to give that up. I wondered what kind of girl did he think I was. Did my looks make him think I would. I was more afraid of what my mother would do to me if she found out I had sex. He tried and tried, but it never happened. I knew how to kiss and that was all I was willing to do. He wanted more than kisses, because the more we were together he started rubbing and touching me all over. I must admit, it did feel good. I felt bad for him, because I knew I was not going to give in. He thought if he was persistant I would. My fear of my mother was stronger than my fear of losing him. I was actually getting bored with him, because it seemed like sex was the goal everytime we got together. He tried his hardest to wear me down and convince me he was a good guy. He would bring his cousins with him when he came over my house to visit. His cousins were nice and we got along well, but I didn't want to see them all the time. Mr. Nice Guy was starting to get on my nerves. I guess I wasn't ready to have a steady boyfriend, because I still wanted to go to the club with my friends. So I told him me and my friends were going out. He wanted to go with me, but I told him it was a girls night out event, and we were just going out to dance and have some fun. This was the night I met John #2.

Chapter 3

John #2 was a very good dancer. I spotted him on the dance floor and I was hoping he would ask me to dance. A couple of songs later he did. His fast dance was better than his slow dance. We danced for a couple of songs. As I was dancing with other guys I could see him out of the corner of my eye watching me. I knew I had gotten his attention. He stood near my table for the rest of the night. He never asked anyone else at my table to dance, only me. The next time we danced he introduced himself and asked for my telephone number. I agreed to give it to him, but he didn't have a pencil or pen to write it down. He said he would be back when he got one. He asked me not to leave without giving him my number. As I thought about it, I was hoping he didn't find one and I would leave. Well, he found one and I gave him my correct telephone number. We danced a few more times and I really liked dancing with him. I could dance just as good as him, and we made each other look good on the dance floor. He told me he liked the way I moved. There was something about him that made me think I should have given him a fake telephone number. I felt he was too old for me and he might be more than I could handle. My friends and I had another good time at the club. John #2 called me a couple days later. Even though I was talking to John #1, I didn't feel like I was cheating on him, because I was just having fun. I let John #2 come over and as soon as he saw me he asked me how old was I. I guess seeing me in different lighting (sunshine) gave him a better view of me, and the fact that when he pulled up I was sitting on the porch with my mother. I told him I was 17. In my mind I hoped he would say I was too young for him and he would turn around and leave. But he didn't. All he said was "young stuff." He told me I was built like a brick house and no one would believe I wasn't older. I don't remember how much I told him about me. It didn't make a difference with him whatever I told him. I think at that moment he had made up his mind that he was going to conquer this young stuff. I knew then it wouldn't be long before sex came into the picture. My mothers response to him let me know she knew he was too old for me, and she didn't really care for him. He only came over once. The only time I would see him is when he came to the club. He called me a few times. I was talking to him and John #1. John #1 did not go to the club anymore, so when I would go and see John #2 at the club I would dance with him throughout the night. When he saw me he would whisper in my ear, "young stuff" and we both would laugh. One night at the club there was a big fight outside and everyone was talking about the guys involved. I think John #2 was one of the guys because after that night he never came back to the club and I didn't see him or hear from him. I was still seeing John #1, and I remember thinking to myself, "I need some excitement". The weekend rolled around and me and the group went to the club. This was the night I met Jerome Adams. When I left the club that night I had already made up my mind that I was going to drop John #1.

Chapter 4

I remember the first time Jerome called. I was so excited I really did not know what to say to him. I never really had a conversation with a man. I had only talked to boys and if it wasn't a yes or no question I really did not know what to say. John #1 did a lot of the talking and I mostly listened. Jerome asked to see me, but I couldn't let him come over because I had not dropped John #1 and I didn't want them to run into each other. I told him he couldn't come that day because I had a lot to do and I would not be at home. That was partly true. What I had to do was break up with John #1. I had never been in a situation like this. I really liked the sound of his voice and I just wanted him to keep talking. I felt comfortable with him. I was able to hold up my end of the conversation. He never asked me how old I was and I was glad so I wouldn't have to lie. He said he was going to college. He told me he lived with his grandmother because he did not want her to be all alone. We talked about things we liked to do and places we'd like to go. He asked me when could he come over and I told him to call me the next day and I would let him know. Later on that day John #1 called and I asked him to come over. When he came over he had a couple of his cousins in the car with him. I guess he thought we would all go somewhere together. He didn't know I asked him over so I could break up with him. I told him I needed to speak with him alone. So he asked his cousins to stay in the car and we went into the house to talk. I told him I did not want to date him anymore because he really made me uncomfortable always trying to get me to have sex with him. I told him I had never had sex. I told him I was not ready for that kind of relationship and I think he needs to find someone who is. He looked totally shocked when he heard that. He said because of the way I looked, he just assumed I was sexually active. He told me he was sorry for making me feel that way, and he would not try anymore. He said he would wait for me to let him know when I was ready. He asked me not to break up with him for that reason, because it would no longer be a problem. I told him I had made up my mind and I think it would only get worst because he wanted to and I didn't. He looked so hurt I almost changed my mind. I thought about Jerome and I didn't change my mind. John #1 pleaded with me not to do this because he really liked me. We hadn't been dating that long, only a little over a month. I guess I didn't realize how much he liked me. I was young and I was only trying to have a good time. I reminded him that his cousins were waiting for him. I couldn't give in or back down. He went to his car and he said something to them. I guess he must have told them what was going on. He turned to come back to the house and his cousins told him to get in the car. I felt bad. I didn't want to hurt him or make him look bad in front of his cousins, but I thought he was coming over by himself. I did not come back outside. He got into his car and sped off. He called me the next day and asked if we could talk about what happened. I told him I was not changing my mind and I think he should find someone who is willing to have sex with him, because I'm not. He still insisted that he could wait for me to be ready. He said I made him feel like he was a monster trying to have his way with me. He said he was a nice guy and he would never hurt me. I told him I believe him, but I'm just too young for him and he needs someone his own age. I told him I was sorry that I let things go on as long as it did. I told him he just need to forget about me. That was our last conversation.

Chapter 5

I thought about John #1 and what had happened. I wondered if the same thing was going to keep happening with every guy I met. I was not ready to have sex. My mother was my deterrent. I knew if she ever found out I was even thinking about having sex, she would kill me. I was too scared. Jerome called and I let him come over. I was looking out the window when he walked up the steps onto the porch and rang the doorbell. I was so excited I thought I was going to faint. He looked so fine to me. He had a smile that made me feel weak in the knees. His eyes were bright and inviting. He had a big afro and a slim body with long legs. He made me feel warm inside. I thought he was so cool. He had on his letterman jacket from his high school. I just wanted to melt. He met my mother, brother, nephew and my sister, who he remembered seeing at the club the night we met. We sat on a sectional sofa in a corner off the living room so we could have some semi privacy. I was the baby girl and there was no way my family was going to let him be all alone with me. I didn't care, I just wanted to be with him. He didn't mind either. We laughed and talked and learned a little more about each other. Eventually my brother left with his friends and my sister went upstairs to talk on the phone, and my mother went to sit on the porch. Then I got my first kiss from him. It was a good one. I can still feel it. My nephew was playing with his toys and several times he would come and stand in front of us and Jerome would play with him. I guess my nephew sensed that Jerome was a good person so he went outside with my mother. I looked at him and I remember thinking to myself wondering how long will it be before he try to have sex with me.

Was I going to have to fight him off too. He asked me how long had I been going to the club. I told him I had been going for a few months. He asked me why I didn't have a boyfriend and I asked him why he didn't have a girlfriend. We both laughed. He told me the night we met was his first time coming to the club. He said he really didn't want to go but his friend talked him into going. He said when he came in he looked all around the place and when he saw me he zeroed in on me for a while. Then he decided he wanted to dance with me. In my mind I said I'm glad he did. He said he told his friend that I was the woman he wanted to be with. That was the beginning of our journey. His visit was a few hours, then he gave me another one of his sweet kisses and he left. After he left I finally came down off the clouds. I called my girlfriend and told her everything that happened. I was still a giggly 17 year old. I really liked him. He came over numerous times and we talked on the phone often too. One night he came over and we went down to the basement to talk and things got really hot. We started kissing and it turned into a lot of rubbing and touching. He was pressing his body against my body real hard. It felt good, but I had to ask him to stop. I was feeling real strange and I didn't know what it was I was feeling. I told him we had to stop because my mother was upstairs and she might come down. He had gotten so excited that his penis was erect and he busted a nut in his pants. I didn't know what to say or do. I thought he would be mad at me, but he said, "That's okay. Don't worry about it. I'll be alright". He wasn't mad and I was shocked. He didn't seem surprised when he found out I was still a virgin. My girlfriends didn't even know I was still a virgin because I had them thinking I had been having sex with other boys. No one knew because of the way I looked. I'm sure my mother knew. Mothers know everything. He didn't try to force the issue, he let it go. I thought that was a good sign. He made me feel comfortable with him. I liked him more for that. Before he left he had to pull his shirt out over the front of his pants so he could walk down the street. He had to ride the bus home. He didn't have a car at that time. I remember Jerome telling me he was going to college. However, he didn't tell me which college. I was going to Highland Park High School and he was going to Highland Park Community College. The buildings were connected. I remember one day me and my girlfriends were hanging out in front of the school in between classes. I was looking around and I looked right in the face of Jerome. I ran back in the school hoping he did not see me. My girlfriends came running inside and asked me what was going on. I told them I just saw the guy that I met at the club and he does not know I am in high school. They laughed. I was frantic. If he saw me I did not know what I was going to say to him. If he didn't see me, I knew it would only be a matter of time before he found out. All that day I was trying to figure out what to do. I knew I was going to see him again and I would know if he saw me. The next time he came over he had a huge grin on his face. I knew then that he saw me. He informed me that he had seen me several times. He said he was waiting to see what and when I was going to say something. So I told him I was 17. He said when we met he thought I was the same age as he was. There was only a two year difference and he did not make a big deal about it. He still wanted to see me. He said I did not look 17 and that is why I was able to get into the club without having to show any ID. So the truth was out and I felt better. He knew the whole story. I still wanted to see him too.

Chapter 6

Jerome and I kept seeing each other. I was young and I still wanted to go to the club with my friends. The weekend came and I told Jerome I was going out with my friends and we were going to the club. When I got to the club Jerome was there and he looked a little displeased with me. He now had gotten himself a car. We spoke to each other, but he did not ask me to dance. I thought that was strange. To my surprise John #2 walked in the door and I didn't know what to do. I grabbed my girlfriend hand and pulled her into the restroom. She didn't know what was going on. I told her Jerome and John #2 were at the club and I didn't know what to do. I had been seeing Jerome on a regular basis, and the last time I saw John #2 he was trying to get with me too. It was a hectic night. John #2 would ask me to dance, and then Jerome would ask me to dance. I made a lot of trips to the restroom that night. My girlfriend laughed at me, but I failed to see the humor in the situation. In between the two of them asking me to dance, I also danced with other guys. This was one night that I wanted to end quickly. When the last call for drinks was made and the lights came on, I quickly made my way to the door to leave. I was already outside standing by the car by the time my group came out the door. I watched Jerome and John #2 go to their cars and leave. It looked like they were looking around for me. Jerome called me two days later and he asked to come over. I let him come over, but he seemed to have something on his mind. He asked me to come and go for a ride with him. I didn't see anything wrong with that, so I went. He asked me if I had a good time at the club, and I thought we were going to get into an argument. I said I always have a good time at the club because I go there just to dance and not to hook up with anyone. We were riding for a while and then he pulled over and parked. I looked around to see where we were and he started to get out of the car. I asked him why was he getting out and where were we going. He told me to just follow him. When I got out of the car and I saw where he was going, I got scared. He had parked right in front of a place called "Tip Motel". I didn't know what to do. Should I run, but where would I go. I didn't recognize the area. If I go in, what do I do. He told me he had a room there, so I thought he meant that he lived there, so I went in. When I got inside I started looking around, I was expecting to see his belongings. I didn't see any of his things, like clothes, shoes or personal items. I said in my mind, "Oh Shit". He could tell I had never been to or in a motel before, because I just stood by the door and I didn't move. He told me to stop standing and sit down. I sat on a chair by the window. He laughed and asked me to come sit beside him on the bed. I was really scared. He told me he brought me here because he really liked me and he wanted to make love to me and he felt it was time. I told him I didn't know what he wanted me to do. He told me if I really liked him then I should trust him. He told me he would take his time and be very gentle with me because he did not want to hurt me. He started to undress and I just sat there with all of my clothes on watching him. When he took off his underwear my heart almost stopped. I could see that he was very well endowed with penis. I said to myself, "He will never get all of that in me, no way". He asked me to take my clothes off and lay down on the bed. I slowly took off each piece of my clothes, and he patiently waited. I sat down on the bed and he sat beside me and put his arms around me and eased me down on the bed. As he got on top of me he told me this was going to hurt, so I could hold his hand and try to relax. He told me to keep looking at him. He gave me a few kissed and then he tried to penetrate me. He was right, it hurted like hell. I let go of his hand and I was trying to push him off of me. He felt me pushing him, and he told me to stop resisting and just let it happen. I tried. I was groaning, but not for pleasure, it was for pain. He stopped and asked me if I wanted to keep on going. He told me to try not to tense up. I took a deep breath and told him I was alright. I told him I couldn't help it. He tried again. It still hurted like hell. I really wanted to do it. I tried to relax, but I couldn't. Tears started building up in my eyes and he saw I was about to cry. He knew I was in real pain, so he stopped. I was also bleeding. He said he could see it was too painful for me, and the more I tensed up the more it was going to hurt. He said he did not want to hurt me. He told me he thought I was ready, but it was okay and we should get cleaned up and get dressed. I thought for sure he was going to be mad at me and I would probably never see him again. He gave me a kiss and said, "I want you to remember I was your first". During the drive back home I was scared my mother would know what we tried to do. Mothers know everything. I told myself pain or no pain I better make sure I am not walking funny when I get out of this car. When I got home I got out of the car and I slowly walked to the porch and sat down on the steps. Jerome came and sat beside me. My mother and sister were sitting on the porch talking to one of our neighbors. Jerome stayed for a few minutes and then he told me he had to go, but he would be back. He surprised me because he called me the next day to see if I was alright. I told him I was not hurting anymore and he said he was glad. I was too young to realize he was the kind of man I needed. Someone who really cares about me and my well being.

Chapter 7

Jerome kept telling me that he really liked me, but I did not understand just how much he liked me. I thought since we both were still young it would change, and we are just having fun now. I knew I liked him too. Our relationship changed, it got more intense. One day Jerome picked me up and he took me to his house. I thought I was going to meet his family, but no one was home. So we somehow wound up upstairs in his bedroom. I knew what this meant. He wanted to try to have sex with me again. I was nervous because I thought what if his family came home and caught me in bed with him. What kind of impression would that make. They would think I was some kind of whore. He knew they would not be coming home anytime soon, so they would not be walking in on us. There was no fore play, he just went straight for the vagina. I still tensed up when he got on top of me. Once again he tried, but he still did not penetrate me. He got so excited about having me in his bed, he exploded on my leg and it ran onto the bed. I guess he was just happy I wanted to do it, which meant I must really liked and trusted him. He gave me a towel so I could clean up and get dressed. We went downstairs and talked for a while and then he took me home. I thought to myself, this is the coolest guy I have ever seen. Twice he tried to have sex with me and when it didn't happen he did not get mad or want to stop seeing me. I still did not grasp the extent of his feelings for me. In my mind I asked myself, if he felt this way about me and we haven't had sex yet, what is he going to feel for me when we do have sex. The next time he picked me up he took me over to his friends house. His friend was the one who talked him into going to the club the night we met. His friends parents were not at home, and he and Jerome was in a corner whispering about something. I was sitting on the sofa just looking around. They had a beautiful house. His friend said he had to make a run and he told Jerome to stay until he got back. I thought that was strange. I soon found out what they were whispering about. Jerome led me upstairs to his friends bedroom. I did not like that idea. I felt like a real whore and I was sure his friend must have thought the same thing about me. I told Jerome I did not want to do this at his friends house because it would make me look bad. He told me his friend knew how much he liked me and he really wanted us to get together. He said his friend understood that he didn't have his own place, so he told him he could use his room anytime because both of his parents worked and they were always out. This didn't make me feel any better, but I liked him and I was willing to try again. Still no fore play. Once again he tried, and needless to say I really tensed up. He did not penetrate me and he exploded on my leg again. I told myself, either my hole must be closed or he don't know what the hell he is doing. I felt disappointed this time. I really wanted it to happen. So we cleaned up and went downstairs to wait for his friend to come back. When he came back I couldn't look him in the face. I felt so embarrassed. He and Jerome embraced each other, which I hoped meant we were leaving. Jerome said "Thanks", and we left. His friend waved good bye to me and I waved back, still not looking him in the face. When we got in the car, I told Jerome how uncomfortable that was for me and I told him to never put me in that kind of situation again. He apologized and said he just wanted to make love to me so bad and he didn't want to take me to another motel. He said he wanted it to be in familiar surroundings. I was still a virgin, but he was trying his best to change that. I must admit Jerome was persistant to be the first one to penetrate my walls. I kind of wanted him to be the first too. There was one night he came over and everyone in the house seemed to have something else to do that night. My mother went out went with one of her friends, my sister went out with her friends to the club, and even my brother left with his friends. My mother must have really liked Jerome for her to leave me alone with him. I stayed home to babysit my nephew. As soon as we were alone Jerome took me in his arms and we just layed down on the floor. We started kissing. My nephew had fallen asleep on the sofa, but he woke up and he was crying. We kept kissing. My nephew kept crying. He climbed down off the sofa because he didn't see anyone. When he saw me on the floor he crawled over to me. I told Jerome we had to stop because my nephew would not stop crying. I got up and I picked my nephew up and held him in my arms and rocked him until he fell back asleep. Once I laid him down, Jerome laid me down on the floor again. We started kissing again. This time Jerome was moving his hand under my dress and pulling on my panties. He managed to get them off with no resistance from me. He had unzipped his pants and right before he could take out his penis, I heard my mother coming up the steps on the porch. We both jumped up, he zipped his pants and I pulled my dress down. We both ran to the sofa to sit down. I did not have on any panties and I looked to see where they were, but I didn't see them. It was clear my mother was home for the night and our chance to have sex was over. Jerome stayed a little while longer and then he left. I never found my panties that night. I figured Jerome must have taken them as a souvenir. After that night I thought I would be a virgin until I got married and that was a good thing. My husband would be the first man to enter my walls. I was not hinking of Jerome as my husband. I did not know who it would be. I had no idea what kind of twists and turns my life would take.

Chapter 8

It was 1975 and I would be graduating from high school in June. I had been applying to colleges and I got accepted at my top three choices. My girlfriend had also been applying to colleges and she got accepted to three of her top choices. Two of her choices were out of state, but all of mine were in state. We both were worried about getting a roommate that we did not know. When we looked at our choices for colleges, we discovered we had only one college that was on both our list. It was Michigan State University. We both decided to go to MSU and be roommates. We knew the only person we would be comfortable sharing a room with would be each other. We both were happy about our choice. Jerome and I was still dating. I told him I would be starting college in the Fall. I told him I would be attending Michigan State University. I thought he would be happy for me, but instead he got real quiet and I could tell he was sad. He pleaded with me not to go. He said I could go to the local college with him and we could continue to date. I told him I had the opportunity to go to a major university, and I wanted to go away to college so I could experience the whole college scene. He told me if I go away I would forget about him and he would lose me. He said I would not keep in touch with him and he knew I would not come back to him. He said I would change once I got around the college crowd. I told him this is something I wanted to do, and I'm doing it to better myself. I told him I thought he would be happy for me and he would want me to go. He told me how much he really liked me and he would be hurt if I went away. I thought he was being very selfish, because he wanted me to give up my dream for him. I felt he had no right to expect that of me. I told him I had to go, or I would regret it later. I told him I had to find out what my future would be, and he could be a part of my future. He did not handle my decision well. He wrote me a three page letter telling me how he felt about my decision to go away to college. That letter was the most powerful letter I had ever read. He poured his heart out on those pages. Everything that he felt was in those words and I could feel it. That letter broke me down. I read it several times. I actually considered not going, that's how powerful it was. I felt bad for him because I was not trying to hurt him. I was only trying to improve myself. But he felt like I was getting some kind of enjoyment out of hurting him. Jerome was a good guy. I never met anyone like him. He made me feel special when I was with him. He never treated me bad. He was always so patient and kind to me. I can't think of a time when he even yelled or fussed at me. He was always a gentleman, even when he tried to take my virginity. I didn't have any unkind words to say about him. Somewhere between January and June, before I grauated from high school, Jerome and I stopped seeing each other. We didn't have a falling out, we kind of just disappeared from each other. One minute he was there and the next minute he was gone. I left for college that September. I thought about Jerome and wished I could see him before I left, but I didn't. He knew where I was going and I thought maybe he would surprise me one day and come and visit me. He didn't. However, I did get a surprise visit from John #2. I don't know how he found me. I don't even remember telling him where I was going or what dorm I would be living in. But he found me and I really was not happy about it. He had come all that way to see me so I didn't want to be rude to him in front of my roommate. I also did not want to be alone with him. My roommate thought I did, so she took her pillow and blanket and went to stay with one of our other friends in the dorm. I wanted to stop her but I didn't want John #2 to think I was scared of him, so I let her go. As soon as she was out of the room he let me know exactly what he came for. Sex! Everything was happening so fast I couldn't think fast enough to get out of that situation. I knew the time had come that I was going to have to give up my virgin status. He started taking off his clothes and I started taking off mine too. I told myself I could do this. I was scared as hell. What if I didn't do it right and he didn't like it. Would he talk about me to his friends. I took a deep breath and laid down on my bed. I closed my eyes real tight and clenched my fist. I was trying to relax so I wouldn't tense up. I felt him get on the bed and then he climbed on top of me. I said in my mind, "This is it". I lay there waiting to feel him try to penetrate me. I was anticipating all the pain I was going to feel. I told myself to just take it like a big girl. I was waiting to feel the pain. I didn't feel anything, but I kept my eyes closed because I didn't want them to fill up with tears, and he would see me crying like a baby. I was still waiting for the pain. Nothing. Then I heard him breathing really hard and something was dripping on me. I opened my eyes. He was actually in me and he was pumping in and out of me, and sweating like a pig. I said in my mind, "He is doing it, but why don't I feel it". My next thought was I needed to be making some kind of sound to let him know I am taking part in this. I was so upset because I realized at that moment I was going to have to fake like I was enjoying it. I guess he reached his climax and he exploded in me and on the bed. I was so disappointed, I don't think I came at all. When he rolled over onto the bed, I said to myself, "Get off me and get out". I felt so cheated, because he was the first person to actually penetrate me and I didn't feel it. Where was the pain that would turn into pleasure? Where was the blood that would be mixed with sperm? I was robbed and I was not happy about it. We both cleaned up and he left. I was so gald he did not want to spend the night. But this was not my night, because he came back. His car had a flat tire and he needed to call his friend to come and get him. He couldn't reach him, so he had to spend the night. I did not want him to touch me, but the bed was only a twin size. He slept with his arms and legs wrapped around me. I was miserable the whole night. The next morning he contacted his friend and he met him at his car. I missed a couple of classes by the time his friend got there. I was not happy about that either. I don't remember if I kissed him good bye. I just wanted him to leave. I thought about Jerome and how he made me feel everytime we were together. I did not feel good with John #2. He made me feel cheap. I promised myself he would never touch me again. I kept that promise. However, I do remember one time when I went home for a visit and some how he found out I was in town. He came by my house and asked me to go for a ride with him. I got in the car and he drove me straight to his apartment. I went inside with him. He came up to me and put his arms around me and asked if we could have sex. The thought of doing it with him again turned my stomach. I told him I didn't come there for sex. I thought we were going for a drive. He locked his arms around me and wouldn't' let me go. I told him to let me go and I wanted to leave. He wouldn't take no for an answer, so he tried to unfasten my pants. I slapped his hand away. He kept tugging at my pants trying to pull them down. We were in a full wrestling match. I couldn't believe he was doing this to me. I kept telling him I didn't want to do it, but he kept trying to force me. While we were wrestling I looked around and saw a clock radio on the table. I reached for it and I had it in my hand and I was about to hit him over the head with it. He looked up and saw the radio about to come down on his head. He grabbed my arm and he realized I was not playing. He released his grip on me and I told him to take me home. On the drive home I didn't say anything to him. When I got out of the car I didn't even look back at him. That was the last time I saw John #2.

Chapter 9

I'm in college now and it's time to grow up. Me and my roommate met a lot of people. On campus there was an organization called the Black Caucus. It was put together for the sake of uniting all the black students in the dorms and across the campus. Each dorm had its own chapter. We would come together to discuss campus life for minorities. Thru this organization I met John #3. We lived in the same form. He was from Detroit and I was from Highland Park. He went to the same high school that Jerome went to. I thought about Jerome and wondered what he was doing or where he was. John #3 and I dated all four years of my college life. The first time we had sex I finally felt something. It wasn't painful and I discovered that I really liked sex. We were young so we had sex almost every night. Our four years were very eventful. John #3 was an intelligent and well dressed young man. He taught me how to dress. He had a perm and he was bow legged. We became part of an inner circle that consisted of 8 people. We all became good friends and we all attended all the campus parties together. Before the first semester was over, John #3 and I was a couple. I thought about Jerome. I had left a boy who really cared about me, and at that time I didn't know how to express my feelings for him. What made me think I was ready for a serious relationship. Our friends knew it was going to happen. Being a college student and having a boyfriend was a lot of work. It was not easy. I was putting more attention on my boyfriend than I was on my studying. I almost flunked out of college. My grades had gotten so low, I was put on Academic Probation. When my grades did not get better the next semester I was sent home and told I had to prove to the college that I was serious about my studying. I was told I had to go to my local college for one year and pass all my classes with nothing lower than a 3.0 average. I felt like a failure. I thought I was going to lose my boyfriend as well. I enrolled in the local college and for my first semester I took five classes, a full load. I also had to make sure all the credits from those classes would transfer to MSU. I visited my boyfriend every weekend, and I stayed with him in his dorm room. His roommate would stay in a room with their other friends. We also wrote to each other every week. I passed all my classes. I had four 4.0 and one 3.0 grades. I was allowed to return to MSU the very next semester. When I got back to MSU I was on a serious mission to graduate and never get sent home again. I went to Summer School every year until I graduated. I learned to balance boyfriend and studying. I later found out that while I was away from MSU, John #3 had started going out to clubs off campus with his friends. When I came back to campus he was still going out, but he was telling me he was going to the library to study. I don't know why he felt he had to lie to me, I knew I wasn't his mother. I could tell something was different about our relationship, but I just couldn't put my finger on it. I did notice that every since I got put on Academic Probation and came back, John #3 started acting like he was better than me because his grades never went down. But he didn't realize he was part of the reason for my failing. I was putting in just as much work as he was, in working toward his degree. I was proof reading and typing all of his papers, pulling all night study sessions with him helping him prepare for exams. It seemed the closer he got to getting his degree, the more arguments we had. He was always criticizing me. I was more of a secretary to him than a girlfriend. I felt like part of his degree should be given to me, because I worked just hard for it as he did. He really showed me how much he thought of me when he compared his family to my family. He said we were not financially compatible. Once he even blurted out something that I had told him in strict confidence about my father. He said it in front of all of our friends and I was so furious. He said he was only trying to make a point and I shouldn't get so upset. He was showing me who he was but I wasn't seeing it. John #3 graduated before me. He had gotten a job right after his graduation. With John #3 being gone from campus I could now put all of my time and energy on my studies. Now it was his turn to come and visit me. He came every weekend.

I was living in a three bedroom apartment off campus with two of my friends. When we were together I could sense that there was something different. I knew my feelings for him hadn't changed, but there was something different in his behavior toward me. He talked the same, but his actions weren't lining up. I just shook it off like I was just imagining things. I thought we would be together forever, because he saw that I would do whatever I could to help him. One weekend he didn't come. I got a phone call instead. He told me he had met someone and they had been talking. He said nothing had happened, but the reason he was not coming to see me was because he was going out with her that weekend. I was speechless. All I could think of was that he was such a coward because he could have told me this to my face the last time he came to see me. Instead of facing me he took the cowardly way out and called me. I asked him how could he do something like this to me when I gave him the best of me all the time. When I hung up the phone I was in tears. My roommates came running to see what was wrong. I told them what happened and they were furious. I was messed up for weeks and I didn't hear from him. About a month later he called me. He wanted to apologize for what he had done and how he had done it. He said he had made a big mistake and he wanted me back. I must admit I was so hurt that I only wanted the hurt to go away and I felt being with him would make the hurt go away. Stupid decision. He came to see me the next weekend. My roommates were not impressed, but they were nice to him for my sake. He took me out to dinner. We talked and came back to the apartment and made love. We were together again. Time went by and it was time for me to graduate. He came to my grauation with my mother, brother and my brother's girl friend. Right after the grauation he took me out to dinner and it was then that he gave me the final slap in the face. He told me he needed to find someone that was on his financial level. He said dating me was too much of a financial burden. I had already gone thru so much with him and this was what I got in return. I knew then that the guy that I thought was so wonderful was really a First Class Asshole. I really wanted to get back at him, so I told him I was pregnant. I knew it was wrong, but I couldn't think of anything else at that moment. I knew this would certainly get his attention and I wanted him to hurt like he hurt me. His mouth almost dropped to the floor. I thought he was going to cry. His next statements were all about him. He said I had ruined his life and everything that he wanted to do was shot to hell. He said his life was over and how could he face his parents. I was waiting for him to say something about me, but he never did. He was only concerned about himself. I told him to take me home because I needed to think about what I was going to do. He quickly got his keys and took me home. No good night kiss. I told him to give me a few days to think and I would call him. I told him no one needs to know anything until I get back to him. I left him on pins and needles until I called him. I wanted him to feel the hurt that I felt when he dropped me. I said I would let him off the hook, but I should at least get a few dollars before I cut him loose. I know I was being an asshole just like him. I called him and told him I decided not to have a baby right now, because I was just getting ready to start my career. I told him I would have an abortion. I told him an abortion would cost $110 and I could get it in two days. He actually said thank you to me, like I was doing this for him. He said he would pay for it and he would bring me the money the next day on his way to work. I agreed and the next day, just like he said, he brought me the money. He didn't even ask if I wanted him to go with me or if anyone else was going with me. No concern for my well being. I took the money and shut the door. I think I took that money and went shopping. That was the last time I saw John #3. It took me months and months to get over him. I cried every night, but no one knew. I think my mother knew but she never said anything. Every day I would get up and try to hide all the hurt I was feeling inside. He really hurt me. I thought about Jerome and I wondered if this was the pain that he felt when he wrote me that dramatic letter. However, 30 years later I wrote John #3 a letter and told him the truth about the pregnancy. I had to clear my conscience because that lie always nagged at me and I know I am a better person than that.

Chapter 10

I don't know how it happened, but Jerome came by one night. I don't even know how he knew I was back. I was sitting on the porch thinking about how John #3 had hurt me. Jerome drove up. He came and sat down with me and we talked for a while. He asked me to go for a drive with him because he wanted to have some alone time with me. We drove around and we talked. He told me he still liked me and he thought about me. He asked he how things went in college and what was my field of study. I told him I had graduated and my degree was in Elementary Education. He congratulated me and told me I would be a good teacher because I was a kind person. I was still feeling the hurt from John #3 but I always enjoyed being with Jerome. Somehow he knew something was wrong and he asked me if I wanted to talk about it. I told him I would be alright, and I was happy to see him. He told me he thought about me a lot and he said he would like to make love to me. I told him I wasn't in the love making mood. He told me it would make me forget about whatever is troubling me. I told him no. I asked him where was he taking me. He said we would just ride around. He asked me had I ever made love in a car. To me that was a strange question. I said no, and I didn't want to try it. I think he had already made up his mind that the next time we were together he was going to make love to me, and finally penetrate my walls. I really wanted to do it with him the moment I saw him, but not in the back seat of the car. I really needed to feel like someone wanted me. He told me he hoped that he would see me again. He said thru the years he had driven by my house hoping one day he would see me. As he was driving I just climbed over the front seat onto the back seat. He asked me what was I doing. I told him I was thinking about trying out the back seat. He smiled and asked me was I sure I wanted to do this. I told him to just keep driving and I would let him know if I change my mind. I remembered that day at the Tip Motel and how I never got the chance to feel him inside of me. I wanted to feel something good that day. He still liked me after all that time. So I told him to find a spot. He drove around until he found a secluded spot and he parked the car and got in the back seat with me. There was a blanket on the back seat, so I spread it on the seat like a sheet. He gave me one of his sweet kisses and I smiled. He made me feel at ease. I knew I was going to enjoy this, but I wasn't thrilled about being in the car. There was not a lot of room for me to stretch my legs. I had already taken my panties off before he got in the back seat. When he got on top of me we were staring into each others eyes. This time he got inside of me with no problem and it felt so good. At first I was worried about someone seeing us, but when I felt him inside of me I forgot about everything. This time when he exploded it was inside of me. Even though we were on the back seat of the car, Jerome was very gentle and I could feel the care he had for me. Sex with him was not the same as with others. I could feel his heart. I said in my mind, I wish we were on a bed so I could really express myself. In my head I could hear soft music playing, I don't know why. He was happy and I was happy. After that night we never saw or heard from each other again. Once again we just disappeared out of each others life. I don't think Jerome coming by that night was an accident. I really needed to get over the pain I was feeling. I needed to feel that someone still cared about me, and someone wanted to be with me. I wanted to feel desirable to someone, and I wanted someone to take me in their arms and hold me tight. I wanted someone to talk to me like they really wanted to hear what I had to say. Jerome was the person I needed to see that night. He was the only one who could make me feel that way. I never forgot that night and I never will. That was my first and only time of making love on the back seat of a car.

Chapter II

I was teaching in my old school district. I was now a colleague with the same teachers that taught me. Many of them were gone, either by death or retirement. I felt like I was giving back to the community because I came back home to share my knowledge and talent in the same place I grew up. I started teaching second grade in the elementary school I attended as a child, then I moved to Adult Education. I felt it was also time for me to move out on my own. I was a Teacher, a professional. I moved out of my mothers house. Me and my girlfriend rented a two bedroom apartment. My job was going good and I was ready to go back to the clubs. Me and the group got together and headed out to the club. We started going to a different club. It was called The Jazz Workshop. I met John #4. He was a tall handsome man, and he was a smooth dancer. I liked the way he moved on the dance floor, and I guess he liked the way I moved on the dance floor because he asked me to dance. We dance together quite a few times that night. I danced all night, song after song, with other guys. I would take a sip from the one drink that I ordered and my fingers were starting to blister again. There was no love connection that night. The week went by and the weekend rolled around. We went to the club and John #4 was there. As soon as he saw me he asked me to dance. We danced several times, and this night he asked me for my telephone number. I was ready to start dating again, so I gave him my correct number. He called me the next day and I let him come over. We sat and talked for a while. He didn't stay too long. The next time he came over he asked me to go for a drive with him. He drove a corvette. I had never rode in a corvette before so I was curious about how they drove. He took me to a park and we parked by the water and talked. I felt myself struggling to keep the conversation going. I remember saying to myself, it should not be this hard to talk to someone. I remembered my conversations with Jerome, we never had a problem talking. I always enjoyed talking to him. I learned a few things about John #4 and he learned a little about me. I found out he didn't live too far from my mother and he lived with his parents. I don't remember what kind of job he had, I'm sure I asked. We left the park and I guess he felt it was time to do something else. He asked me if it would be alright if we got a room. I knew what that meant, it didn't make sense to me, but I agreed. He took me to a motel. I said to myself, going for a drive must be the new way to say I want to have sex with you. I wandered what kind of woman did he think I was, so I asked him. He said he did not think of me as a whore, he said he wanted to make love to me the first time he saw me, and he hoped I felt the same way about him. I lied and said I did too. We took our clothes off and laid down on the bed and he went right to work. He did some things to me that I had never had done to me before, but I liked it. We was there for a couple of hours, and then it was over. I wasn't sure what I was suppose to feel. It felt weird. We cleaned up and got dressed and he took me home. For the rest of the night I thought about what had happened. I didn't know if I should feel happy or sad. I knew something was missing, but I didn't know what it was. I just wanted to continue having a good time like I did when we went to the clubs. We continued to go to the club and I would see John #4, we would dance a few times together, but no conversation. We would get together for sex. I could see this was going no where. The sex was the highlight and when it was over there was nothing. Pretty soon he stopped coming to the club. There was no more calls, no more visits. I guess he moved on, and I was fine with that. I learned some new moves from him, on the dance floor and in the bedroom.

Chapter 12

Most of the teachers on staff were former students of the school system. We had weekly staff meetings. Everyone was so nice and friendly. We all got along really well. I met John #5, he was a teacher too. He was a very handsome man. All the women in his class really liked him. They would watch him as he walked down the halls. I had no intentions of dating him. I remember we were planning the annual Christmas Party and everyone was giving their ideas. The party was going to be at one of the teachers house. I didn't have a car, so John #5 offered to pick me up. I thought it was a nice gesture. John #5 had flirted with me a few times in the halls at school, but I didn't think anything about it. The night of the party came and he picked me up. When my roommate saw him she told me I had must be crazy not to be dating him. I don't know why, but I thought there would be other people in the car. It was only him and me. We arrived at the party and all my colleagues were coupled up with their husbands, wives, boyfriends and girlfriends. John #5 and I were unattached. The party was going great. We ate, drank and sang songs. Everyone opened up and told a little about themselves. We became a family that night. The party went late into the night because no one wanted to leave. John #5 had gotten real comfortable and he started hugging me and he kissed me under the mistletoe. The party finally came to an end and everyone started hugging each other and saying their good byes. This went on for about 10 minutes. John #5 took me home. On the drive home our conversation started getting a little more personal. I figured it was the alcohol talking. John #5 was from a well to do family. His parents wanted him to do something else with his life. He wanted to be a teacher and he was proud of his choice. I felt bad when I got out of his car because I wore a Rabbit Skin coat and there was fur all over the seat when I got out of the car, but he didn't say anything. The next day at work everyone was more friendly towards each other. We had bonded at the party. We greeted each other with big smiles. John #5 greeted me with big hugs and kisses (when no one was around). I didn't see this coming. He asked me if I had plans for the weekend because he would like to come over and go swimming with me. I told him I didn't have any plans and he could come over. He kept giving me hugs and kisses all week long. He came over on Saturday. He got in the pool, but I didn't. I didn't want my hair to get wet. I sat on the side of the pool with just my feet in the water. He was so fine. He had a nice body too. I'm sure that's what he wanted me to see. John #5 swam for about an hour, and then he got out of the pool and came inside to shower. I gave him a towel to dry off and he decided he didn't want to dry off at that moment. He wrapped the towel around his waist and walked up to me and gave me a big and wet kiss. He then proceeded to nudge me toward the bedroom as he was kissing me. I knew what he wanted. He didn't have to nudge me too hard because I wanted the same thing be wanted. He looked so good with the water glistening on his perfect body. As we moved toward the bedroom he started undressing me. By the time we got in the bedroom I was completely naked. We fell on the bed and gave each other what we both wanted. No words were spoken, there were only sounds of steamy hot passion. An hour later he was back in the shower cleaning up again. I started to get in the shower with him, but I knew if I did that neither one of us would get clean. The sex was great, but I had that feeling again that something was missing. We only had sex that one day. We both realized we should not have done it, because now it would be difficult working together and remain professional at work. But we were determined to do it. We didn't want our co-workers to know that we had an intimate contact. I believe they knew, I'm sure our body language probably told it all. But no one said anything to us. We worked together for another year. By the next year John #5 was gone. I think he got a job in a high school some where in Detroit.

Chapter 13

Me and my girlfriends went back to the club. The Jazz Workshop had multiple locations, so we went to a different location to see if we would enjoy it. We were having a good time as usual. I was on the dance floor all night as usual, and I occasionally sipped on my drink as usual. I noticed a guy watching me dance, but he never asked me to dance. The following Monday morning I caught the bus to work as usual. The bus driver stopped me as I paid my fare and asked me if I was at the Jazz Workshop on Saturday night. I said I was. He said he was there and he thought he recognized me. He said I was looking real good, and he asked me if I would be there next Saturday. I told him I probably would. He said he would be there and he hope to see me there. I smiled and walked to my seat. I could see him looking at me in the rear view mirror. I smiled and he smiled. This was John #6. I got to my stop and I walked to the front of the bus to get off. He said, "I'll see you Saturday". I said, "I'll see you too". The week couldn't go by fast enough for me. I had already planned on what I would wear. I told my girlfriends and they wanted to see who this guy was. We got to the club and I didn't want to look like I was looking for him. So after we picked our table I went to the restroom. On my way I glanced around the place and I saw him. I acted like I wasn't really looking. He was sitting a couple tables over from me. When I came out of the restroom I made sure he had a full view of me as I slowly strutted to my table. A few songs played before he asked me to dance. It was a slow song, so he got a chance to put his arms around me. For some unknown reason it felt awkward being in his arms. I don't know why, but I felt like we were doing something wrong.

He formerly introduced himself and he asked for my telephone number. I gave it to him. A week had gone by and I had not heard from John #6, so I figured he must have lost my number. I didn't think I would see him again, and that was alright with me. But the next day I was catching the bus to work, and John #6 was the driver. He stopped me as I was paying my fare and told me he had lost my number, and he really wanted to talk to me. He asked if I would give him my number again. I said I would. This time he told me what time he would be arriving at my stop when I got off work. He asked me if I would ride with him to the end of his route. I agreed. I met him at the appointed time when I got off work and I rode with him to the end of his route. He drove the bus to the terminal and asked me to wait for him at his car. He walked me to his car and opened the door so I could wait inside the car for him. I was kind of leary about what I was doing. It took a little while for him to do whatever he had to do, then he came to the car and we drove off. He said he would take me home but he wanted to go by his house first, and I said that would be alright. As soon as I said it I wished I hadn't said it. I didn't really know this guy and I should not be going to his house alone. We got to his house and I saw that it was a nice neighborhood. We go inside and he offers me something to drink. I turned it down. He said he wanted to shower and change his clothes before he took me home. I said it was okay. As I looked around his house I could tell he did not live there alone. There were female belongings all around. I could hear him turn on the shower. He came into the room with only a towel wrapped around him. I knew what that meant. He slowly walked up to me and gently kissed me and asked me to follow him. Of course he was leading me to the bedroom. I saw more female things. When we got to the bed he took his towel off and asked me to join him on the bed. I started taking off my clothes as he watched. I laid down on the bed and he climbed on top of me. It took all of 20 minutes and then it was over. He told me he had dreamed of this moment when he first saw me. I didn't know if I should be flattered or insulted. He went to take his shower and he gave me a towel to clean up. We got dressed and he took me home. I didn't feel special. I don't know what I felt, but it wasn't good. He kissed me good bye and drove off. He must not have gone home because about 2 hours later I got a phone call. I thought it was him, but it was a woman asking for him. I told her she had the wrong number, but she called me by my name and repeated my telephone number. I knew at that moment she was the female at his house. I told her he was not there and she slammed down the phone. I felt really bad. This man had taken me to his house that he shared with another woman, and we had sex in the same bed they slept in together. After that day John #6 never called me again. The next time I saw him at the club he was with a woman and he acted like he didn't know me. I figured that woman with him must have been the woman who called me. I wasn't trying to get into no fight over no man, so I acted like I didn't know him either. I was so mad at myself for doing what I did. Why was I acting like a desparate woman. Why did I let this man disrespect me and the woman he lived with. I felt cheap and humiliated. I was single and I could have any man I wanted. I didn't want someone else man. That's like chewing someone else bubble gum. I could have my own piece. That was not how I do things. I wanted to kick myself. What kind of man was he? Surely he was not the man for me and the woman that he was with also deserves a better man.

Chapter 14

I was really on a roll for making bad decisions, because I was about to make a really big mistake. I was teaching at Adult Education and some of my students were younger than me, some were my age and some were older than me. There was one of my students who had a obvious crush on me. He was younger and I should have left him alone. I was planning to give a Pool Party and I invited him and his friend (who was also my student). Big mistake. They came to the party and most of my co-workers came too. They were surprised to see him there. I told them he was one of my best students. He was John #7. He got the chance to see me outside the school walls and in a swimsuit. His friend met one of my friends and they seem to hit it off. I didn't tell my friend he was a student of mine. Me and John #7 talked a lot. He let me know that he was interested in me. I told him I was not sure it would be a good idea for us to get involved. His reply was that we are both adults and we can do whatever we want. I agreed and we exchanged telephone numbers. The party went very well. Everyone had a good time. The next school day I saw John #7 in the hall in between classes and he told me he wanted to come over. I knew it was a bad idea, but I let him come over. I caught the bus home and he drove his car to my place. Once inside my apartment he said he was curious about my world. He wanted to see what teachers did for entertainment. I thought to myself, is this just a school boy crush or is he just living out a childhood fantasy of having sex with his teacher. We talked and one thing lead to another. After all, he was a younger man that was interested in me, and of course I was flattered and curious too. Something was terribly wrong. He could not get a full erection. He tried to play it off like he was too nervous. We had kiddie sex, which meant he could only rub his penis up against my vagina. He couldn't get hard enough to penetrate me. He came on my leg and the bed. It was a mess. I didn't want him to feel bad so I told him maybe this was a sign for us to slow down and think about this some more. We continued to see each other. We met a couple of times at the club. My friends did not know he was one of my students. The sex never got any better. I thought he must not like me as much as he say he do, or he has a male problem. I found out he had a girl friend and she was probably the reason I couldn't get a full erection from him. I figured by the time he got to me he was already worn out. Then I asked myself why was I allowing someone to make me their second choice. I was no ones second choice. This had to end. The school year was ending and he was graduating, so I wouldn't be seeing him anymore. My mind drifted off and I thought about Jerome. When I was with him I had his full attention. There was no other woman. At the same time I met John #7, my roommate had met a guy and he was coming over every night. She was secretly trying to move him in. Everytime he came over he would bring a change of clothes, but I never saw him take any clothes out. I knew it was time for me to have my own space. So rather than fall out as friends with my roommate, we both agreed we needed to have our own apartment. We moved out of the two bedroom apartment and we both got our own one bedroom apartment. We lived in the same apartment complex, we just chosed different buildings. All of the furniture in our apartment belonged to my roommate. All I had was a bed, a dresser and a television. I didn't care, I just wanted my own space.

Chapter 15

I was enjoying my own space. It didn't matter to me that I didn't have a place to sit, I would sit on the bed or the floor. I started buying furniture one piece at a time. The first piece I bought was a Dinette Table with chairs. I got tired of eating on the floor or eating on my bed. I would take my time and shop around for the furniture for my living room. The apartment complex that I lived in was only about one mile from a major mall, which was perfect for me because I loved to shop. One day while I was at the mall a guy came up to me and spoke to me by my name. I was surprised because he looked familiar to me. Then I remembered where I met him. He was at the Christmas Party, but he was with one of my co-workers. They was all hugged up together when I met him. I thought he was at the mall by himself. He was checking me out. I didn't remember his name and he could tell, so he told me his name again. He asked me if I was shopping by myself. I told him I was. He said he was there with his daughter and she was inside the store we were standing in front of. He said he would like to talk to me and he gave me his telephone number. I asked him about my co-worker that he was seeing. He told me they had a falling out. He was a big thick handsome man. I thought to myself, she must be crazy. He was John #8. I didn't want to seem too anxious so I waited a couple of days before I called him. He was happy when I called. The first thing I asked him was if he and my co-worker had gotten back together. He said no. He asked if he could take me out to dinner and I said yes. He came over and when I opened the door I told him I didn't have any furniture, so there was no place to sit. He didn't say anything. We went to an Italian

Restaurant. The food was delicious. We talked as we ate. He was a Teacher too. He taught at the high school and he was also the Football Coach. He was divorced and he had two children and they lived with him. I learned a little about him and he learned a little about me. There was another side to him, and I would learn about that side further down the road. After dinner we went back to my apartment. I asked him if he mind having to sit on the floor and he said it was alright with him. The conversation took a different route. He told me he was attracted to me when he met me at the Christmas Party. He said he was having a hard time trying to keep his attention on his date. He asked me if he could kiss me. I had never been asked for a kiss, so I told him yes. It was a long tongue thrusting kiss and I liked it. One kiss led to another and another and another. Soon the hands started moving. He was rubbing my back, then my ass, then my thighs, then my inner thighs and then he went for the vagina. I grabbed his hand. He didn't stop kissing me. He tried again. This time I stopped kissing him. He said he couldn't help himself. He said he had been wanting to do that ever since he saw me at the mall. He asked me if I would let him make love to me. I told him no, it was too soon because we had just officially met. He said he understood, and then he asked me if we could just touch each other. He said he just wanted me to hold his penis in my hand for a minute. I thought that was strange, but I agreed. I was curious too. He put his hand down my pants and into my panties and pushed his finger into me. It felt so good I almost changed my mind about having sex with him that night. He unzipped his pants and took out his penis and I know my eyes got big, because it was big and long. I wrapped my hand around it and he moaned. I gave him a few strokes and he asked me if I had changed my mind about having sex with him. In my mind I said, "Hell yes", but my mouth said no. We stroked each other for about another minute and then I said we had better stop. He agreed and we both fixed our clothes and he gave me another hot passionate kiss and he asked me for my telephone number, and then he left. I was glad he left, because he didn't know how close he came to getting me to change my mind. A week later he called and I let him come over. This time the answer was yes. I still didn't have any living room furniture, but we only needed the bed. I was about to learn about the other side of him. The sex was amazing. He was very vocal. He asked me to talk dirty to him, he said it made him hot.

I really didn't know how to talk dirty, no one had asked me to do that. I tried. He was gentle, then he really got into it and he got more aggressive. I liked it. But then he started getting a little rough and I had to tell him to calm down. He told me some of the things he liked to do, but some of them were too wild for me. I did not want to do some of those things and he didn't try to force me. Some of the things he wanted me to say to him was things I couldn't bring myself to say. John #8 was a little too freaky for me. The sex lasted for several hours. I was tired and he was tired. We had to rest before we could get ourselves together. He got dressed and he left. The more we talked on the phone his conversations were getting more and more obscene. I started losing interest in him. Once again I thought about Jerome. He never talked to me the way this man was talking to me, and I know I turned him on. Jerome was always a gentleman to me. This guy made me feel dirty. I eventually asked him to stop calling me because he was making me feel uncomfortable and his conversations were too graphic for me. He said some really disgusting things to me, but he thought he was being sexy. He said he knew his behavior could seem scary, but that was the way he was. He said he had a very explicit imagination. He said he liked to act out his fantasies no matter how wild they may be. It's too bad we didn't work out. I must admit he was the most hot, intense, passionate and highly aroused lover I had ever had. He made my toes curl. But John #8 was too much for me. Now I understood why my co-worker stopped dating him. I stopped seeing him too.

Chapter 16

It was now 1984. A lot had happened in my life, but the journey wasn't even half way over. I've only scratched the surface. The deep things hadn't happened yet. I was still teaching Adult Education and I loved it. My classes were full and my students were very cooperative. One student in particular gave me all of his attention. He sat in the front row in class. He would linger after class, and watch me as I walked down the halls. He would compliment me everytime he saw me and offer to carry my books and packages. He was trying to be the Teachers Pet. My brothers' birthday was coming up and I was giving him a Surprise Pool Party. I invited that student who became John #9. I was still making bad decisions. I introduced him as a friend of mine. He was a few years older than me. After the party was over everyone went home except John #9. We talked for a while and then we had amazing sex. We were going strong for about 2 hours. I knew I should not have allowed this to happen, but I figured we were adults and we could handle this. That's what I thought. I let him move in with me and everything changed. John #9 behavior in class changed. He started slacking off in class, and not doing all his assignments, not taking tests and coming to class late. I told him he was still a student and he still had to do the work. He said he would do the work. I soon found out our secret relationship was not a secret anymore. He was bragging to his friends and other teachers that he was banging my brains out and I would help him get his diploma. He was causing conflict with me and my co-workers. I realized I had made a big mistake and my creditability as a teacher was on the line. I was called in the office by the Director of the program. He asked me if I was having a problem controlling my classes. I knew what he meant and I assured him I would get everything under control. In the short time that we messed around John #9 had the nerve to try to be possessive. He acted like he owned me and that really turned me off. I knew I had to get rid of him. During this time I had applied for a job with another company that was paying much more money than I was making as a teacher. Graduation was also coming up. John #9 did the work for his other classes and I passed him in my class. I wanted him to be out of the program so I wouldn't have to see him when I got rid of him. The next semester began and mid way into the semester I received a call from the other company I applied to, and I had an interview. I passed the interview and I received another call while I was at work telling me I was hired and I was to report to the company in two weeks. I was excited and sad. I was sad because this meant I would be leaving my chosen field of teaching. I was going to miss the students and my co-workers. I was excited because I was going to make much more money and I would have more opportunities to do other things in the company. I began working at Blue Cross Blue Shield of Michigan on November 26, 1984. I was still living with John #9, and I began planning my get away. I wasn't leaving him just because I got a new job. I was leaving him because he had been cheating on me. There was some girl who kept calling my apartment and when I would answer the phone she would hang up. I asked him about it but he claimed he didn't know who it was. I had my telephone number changed several times and still she called. I guess he thought I was that stupid and I would believe anything he told me. I went looking for another apartment. I found one in the heart of downtown. It was a few blocks away from the company where I would be working. It was perfect. I didn't tell John #9 the correct location of the apartment. I told him it was on the west side of town and it was bigger. He was happy that we would be moving. On the day that I was moving I told John #9 that I needed him to stay at the old apartment to wait for them to do the exiting inspection. I told him I would be at the new apartment setting everything up and I would come back and get him. He agreed. When I pulled off from the old apartment in the truck, I exhaled a sigh of relief. I never saw John #9 after that day. I wonder how long it took him to realize I wasn't coming back to get him. He would also find out I did not tell him the truth about the new apartment, so he wouldn't know where I was. I told myself I have got to start making better decisions. I was looking for something, but I didn't know what I was looking for. Whatever it was I did not find it in any of the guys that I had dated thus far.

Chapter 17

I liked living Downtown. Everything was in walking distance. I could walk and go shopping. I could walk to the Riverfront and attend the Summer Festivals. I could walk to the Movies. I could walk to my choice of restaurants and I could walk to work. My apartment was on the 16th floor and the building also had a store, a bar and a restaurant on the main floor. The Grocery Store was not in walking distance, I would have to get a ride to go grocery shopping. I still did not have my own car. On the weekends I would go shopping. One day after a shopping trip I was on my way back to my apartment and I noticed a bus had pulled over and stopped. I remembered that my brother told me he saw my friend Jerome and he was driving a bus. I immediately thought it was him and he had seen me. As I was approaching the bus the door opened and the driver said, "Hello Miss Lady, you look nice today". I did not recognize the voice and when I turned to see who it was, it was not Jerome. I just smiled and said, "Thank you," and I kept walking. For some reason I thought because I lived Downtown I would run into Jerome one day. I didn't even know which bus route he had. I would have liked to see him again. I never saw him. However, this bus driver kept doing the same thing several more times. Each time he would say something to me as I passed his bus. I guess he saw that I was not going to stop and talk to him, so he tried a different approach. When he opened his door to speak to me he said, "Excuse me ma'am, may I talk to you for a minute, I don't mean you any harm. I have been trying to talk to you but you never give me a chance". I stopped at the door. I told him I don't normally stop and talk to anyone yelling at me. He told me that was his only way to get my attention. He asked me to step inside the bus. I stood on the first step. He told me his name and I told him mine. He said he had seen me numerous times and he really wanted to meet me. He asked if I lived near by and he said he would like us to get together. He asked if we could exchange telephone numbers. So we did. He thanked me for finally stopping and giving him a chance to talk to me. He said he would call me when he finished his shift. I told him that would be fine. I got off the bus and went home. I said to myself I hope he don't think I'm a hooker on the stroll. I don't know why I came to that conclusion. This was John #10. He called me that night just like he said he would. We talked and we agreed to get together on the weekend. The week seemed to go by so fast. John #10 said he would pick me up after his shift. He asked me if it would be alright with me if we got a take-out meal and go back to his place. I was a little hesitant and then I said it would be okay. As I was waiting for him to pick me up I wondered if I should have had him bring the food to my place. I wasn't sure about going to an unknown place with someone I just met. When he picked me up he said he had to make one stop on our way. He said he had to go by his parents house and it would only take a few minutes. I thought to myself, this is kind of early to be meeting his parents. I looked at him and it was very obvious that he was much older than me, so I said his parents got to be senior citizens. We got to his parents house and he asked me to come in with him. This didn't feel right to me. I met his parents, he introduced me a friend. They were very nice. I felt a little more eased. He did what he had to do and we left and went and picked up some food and headed to his place. He lived in a two-family flat and he lived upstairs. When I walked in I saw that he had a cat. I figured a man with a cat is usually very kind and gentle. His cat really liked him because she came running to him when he walked in the door. He reached down and picked her up. That made me feel a little better. I didn't know where I was or how to get home from there. I knew it was on the Eastside. He sat the food on the table and got plates, utensils and napkins. We ate and talked. He turned the television on and after dinner we sat on the couch. The cat sat and watched us. As we talked he kept moving closer and closer to me. When he got as close as he could he told me I should just relax and let whatever happens happen and whatever don't happen won't happen. I was okay with that. He was being very gentle. He gave me a sweet kiss, then he gave me a more passionate kiss with tongue action. I responded and the next thing I knew we were partially naked. He had taken off my clothes and I had taken off his clothes. We finished undressing ourselves and went into the bedroom. The sex was good and during the whole time his cat was sitting on the floor at the door watching us. When I saw her I felt embarrassed. I told him his cat must think I'm too easy because I went to bed with him on my first visit. He told me his cat always watches him while he sleeps and she usually jumps on the bed with him. We cleaned up and he took me home. We got together the next weekend, but this time he came to my apartment. He told me liked to play chess. He asked me if I knew how to play. I told him I always wanted to learn how to play but no one ever taught me. He told me he could explain the game to me. He brought his chess set with him when he came over. Before we got into the game we ate and had sex. He explained each piece to me and I under stood, we played a game. He won of course. But he said for my first game he could feel my game and that was good. I was happy about that. Then he said something that took the thrill out of learning the game. He said he would continue to teach me how to play, but for every game we played I had to have sex with him. John #10 really messed up when he said that. All I could think of was he must think I'm a hooker for real and I'm that cheap that I would give him my body for a game. He can't be for real. I told him I appreciate him giving me the basics of the game, but I would stick to checkers. I was ready for him to leave. He could sense that my countenance had changed and he knew he had messed up. I didn't call him anymore and I guess he knew not to call me either. I never saw his bus stopped on the side of the rode anymore after that day.

Chapter 18

Everything was going good. I really liked my job. On the days when I didn't feel like cooking I would stop at one of the restaurants on my way home and pick up a meal. People at work were friendly and people in my apartment building were friendly. There was a young man in my building who spoke to me all the time, and one day he rode up the elevator with me. He asked me if I was new in the building. He said he noticed me a few times and he thought I was a beautiful lady. I had noticed him a few times. He told me he lived on the 10th floor. He told me his name and I told him mine. He got off the elevator at his floor and he said he hope to see me again. After the doors closed I said to myself he looks too young for me, I better leave that alone. I don't know if he knew my work schedule or if he was following me, but every day he made sure he was in the lobby when I came home. We talked a little more each time I saw him. He said he wanted to be friends with me because he didn't have a lot of friends and sometimes he just wanted someone to talk to. I told him it's good to have someone you can talk to. So we became friends. I would invite him to my apartment and we would have dinner together and watch movies. He finally told me that he lived with his mother. He said she didn't want to live by herself, so he stayed with her to help her out. I wondered about that explanation, but I was only trying to be a friend. I think his mother worked because I never saw her, but I could tell there was a female in the apartment. I asked him how old he was, and he told me he was 19 and he would be 20 on his birthday, which was a few months away. I knew he was young, but not that young. I asked to see his Drivers License. He really was 19. Yes, he was John #11. I told him I was 28 and he might be too young for me. I said I didn't want his mother to have me arrested. He said he was grow and his mother only wants her son to be happy. He said we got along too well for our age to be a problem. He said he was past high school age and it is not a problem for him. He told me he always have liked older women. My mind told me to stop. I told him we had not done anything wrong yet so maybe we should stop before we do. He invited me to his apartment to watch a movie. He offered me a glass of wine. I started not to take it but I did. It was good wine. After I finished my wine I left. I told him I needed to think about this friendship. He told me he hope we can keep seeing each other. I made sure I didn't see him for a couple of days. Then one day he came up to my apartment and knocked on the door. When I opened the door he grabbed me and gave me a big kiss. He said he missed me and he didn't want me to stop seeing him. He asked me to give him a chance to show me he wasn't too young for me. I let him in and he gave me another long and passionate kiss. It was the middle of the afternoon when we went into the bedroom. It was late in the evening when we came out of the bedroom. We had been making love for hours. This young man had amazing stamina, and I guess I did too. I was out of breath when we stopped. I must have really rocked his world because he did not want to stop. I wanted to stop because I had gotten hungry. He was going to light a cigarette but I stopped him and told him I didn't smoke and I didn't allow anyone to smoke in my apartment. He asked if he could go into the bathroom and smoke. I told him no because I would still smell it and I didn't want the smoke to get in my hair, my clothes, or my furniture. I told him he had to go so I could get some rest. He smiled and jumped in the shower. After he got dressed he left. I told myself I knew I was going to regret this. I think I rocked his world a little too much. Sure enough that Monday when I went to work he showed up at my job around noon time as I was going to lunch. He was sitting in the lobby and I saw him and asked him what he was doing there. He told me he wanted to see me and have lunch with me. I told him I had made plans with my friends and we were going out. I told him he can't just show up on my job and expect me to be available for him. I told him he has to let me know in advance if he would like to come and have lunch with me. I left with my friends and I didn't introduce him. He turned around and left. When

I got home from work I didn't see him, but when I got to my apartment there was a rose taped to my door. It was a plastic rose, and it was a dirty plastic rose. I took it off my door and threw it in the trash. A couple hours later I got a knock on my door, it was John #11. When I opened the door he was standing in the hall with a suitcase in his hand. I asked him why did he have a suitcase. He said he had a fight with his mother and he was moving out. He asked me if he could stay with me. I said in my mind I knew I would regret it. I told him whatever he argued with his mother about, he needed to go back and fix it. I told him he should not be fighting with his mother no matter happens. I told him he could not stay with me, I liked living alone. He asked if he could leave his suitcase with me while he go and talk to his mother. I knew that suitcase was his way of trying to get his foot in the door and then he would never leave. I told him he had to take his suitcase with him, and I closed my door. I told myself that's an old trick and I wasn't falling for it. This young man had become clingy. He wanted to be with me all the time. This what not what I wanted. It was clear to me that he wasn't living with his mother to help her out, he had to live with her. He was not going to college, he had no job, no money and no friends. He never moved out on his own. His mother was still taking care of him. We were two different kind of people. I was independant and he was dependant. Not a good mix. I saw him the next day and he told me he had apologized to his mother and everything was alright. I knew that meant he was going to try to find another way to get into my apartment and I wasn't up for the games. He asked if he could come up for dinner. I told him I didn't think it was a good idea for us to keep seeing each other. I told him we could be friends and nothing else. He looked surprised when I said that. He knew at that moment that the game was over and he had lost. After that day I saw less and less of him in the building. Eventually I didn't see him at all. I think they moved out.

Chapter 19

A few months went by and I was in the lobby waiting at the front door for my friends to pick me up. As I was standing by the door a man came out of the bar that was in the building and as he was going out the door he stopped and looked at me and he told me how beautiful I looked. He said he couldn't stop looking at me. He asked me if I was waiting for my husband or my boyfriend. I told him I was not married and I didn't have a boyfriend. He asked me if he could take me wherever I was going. I told him I didn't know him and my friends were on their way. He asked me if he could wait with me so he could talk to me. We were standing in the lobby and there were people going in and out of the store, the restaurant and the bar, so I felt nothing could happen. I asked him what did he want to say to me. He told me his name and he said he was a Detroit Police Officer and he told me which precinct he worked at. He was not in uniform, he had on sweats. He showed me a patch on his sweats that had some kind of emblem for the Detroit Police Department. I told him my name. He said he had been to that bar many times and he had never seen me. He said he would have remembered me if he had. I told him I was new in the building. He asked me if we could meet for drinks. I asked me when did he want to meet. He told me I could pick the day and he wrote down his telephone number and gave it to me. He asked if he could have my telephone number. I told him I would give it to him when I called. He knew why I said that, because he assured me he had given me the right number, and he said is not married and he also did not have a girlfriend. He told me he lived with a roommate, who is a guy. While we were talking my friends finally arrived and I went out the door to get in the car. He said he hoped I call him. I smiled and got in the car. My friends asked me who was the cutie pie I was talking to. I told them I just met him while I was standing at the door and he wants me to call him so we can meet for drinks. They told me if I don't call him give one of them his number and they would certainly call him. We laughed and pulled off. I waited several days before I called him. He knew who I was when he heard my voice. He said he didn't think I was going to call, but he was glad I did. I could hear people talking in the background. He said he and his roommate had some friends over and they were just hanging out. He asked for my telephone number and I gave it to him. Then he asked when could we get together. I told him I would like for him to come over for dinner. He asked what day and what time. It was the middle of the, week so I told him Friday would be a good day. I asked him what time did he get off duty and he said whatever time I wanted him to be there he would be there. I told him to come at 7:00 and he said that was okay. This was John #12. Friday seemed to come real fast. He was ringing my buzzer from the lobby. I buzzed him in and he came up. When I opened the door he had on sweats, it looked like the same ones he had on when we first met. I guess I must have had some kind of look on my face, because he told me he had just gotten off duty and he always wear sweats. He said he had several pair of the same ones, just in case I thought he was wearing the same ones he had on the last time I saw him. We talked a little and then we had dinner. I moved the television into the living room and we watched television and had more conversation. Then he said he think he should leave because it was too soon for anything more to happen. I agreed with him that he should leave. After he left I had a strange feeling that something wasn't adding up. I don't know what it was but my gut kept telling me to be careful. I knew he was a cop and I didn't want him to overpower me, so I knew I had better keep my eyes open and pay attention to everything he say and do. I guess I was a little uneased. The weekend for the fireworks down town was coming up. He called and asked me if he could come over after the fireworks. I told him that would be fine. It rained on that day so the fireworks were delayed. I didn't expect to see him till much later that night. He came earlier than expected. He said due to the rain he got off earlier. I thought that was strange, but I didn't question him. He had on sweats again. He asked me if I had a picture of myself that he could have. I thought that was a strange request, because no one had ever asked me for a picture. I figured he must want it to show to his friends. I told him the only picture I had of myself was my college graduation picture. I showed it to him and he said he would like to keep it. I gave it to him. We had sex that night. It was only okay, nothing to shout about. After we cleaned up and he got dressed, he left. I figured he knew I was not really impressed with his sexual performance. The next day I was talking to my brother and I told him about a guy I had met that said he was a police officer. My brother had friends that were Detroit Police Officers, so he asked me his name and which princt did he work. I told him and he said he would see if his friends knew him. He had friends that worked at the same precinct. My brother called me the next day and told me no one at that precinct knew him and his name was not on any roster they had. I knew then John #12 had lied. I should have followed my gut and let this one go. I told my brother he said he had been transferred there, so maybe that is why they don't know him. My brother said he would ask his friend to check it out. My brother asked me did he show me his badge or any kind of ID. I told him the only thing I saw was the sweats that he wore that had some kind of emblem on them that said Detroit Police Department. He told me anyone can get those. He may have gotten them from someone he knows on the police force. I told him I must be slipping, I let my guard down. I told him not to worry, I got this. He said for me to let him know if there is a problem. John #12 called me, but I didn't let him know what I had found out. I didn't trust him anymore, so when he asked to come over I told him I was going out with my friends. I could hear his roommate in the background and he sounded like he was angry. I asked John #12 what was going on. He told me his roommate had gotten into an argument with his girlfriend and he was really upset. I could hear him fussing but no one was answering him. For some reason I felt the anger was directed at John #12. I wondered if he was a Bi-sexual guy, and he actually swung both ways. I didn't like what I was thinking or feeling. I started pulling away from him until we were not talking or seeing each other anymore.

Chapter 20

At this point I was really tired of meeting the wrong man. I was tired of dating. I was tired of being lied to. I was tired of the games and I did not want to date anymore. I was ready to call it quits and settle down with one man. I was ready to get married. That sounded strange for me, I was only 29 years old. Then one day at work a friend of mine was in the ladies room talking with someone else about her boyfriends' brother. She was saying he was such a nice guy and she wish she could find a nice woman for him, because he has had a lot of bad dates. At that moment I walked into the restroom. She looked around and saw me and said to her friend, "Anita". She asked me if I wanted to meet a really nice guy. I told her I have had my fill of nice guys who turn out to be not such nice guys. I told her I can't take another bad date. She told me this guy would not be like the other guys I had met, he is a good guy. She said he is her boyfriend's brother and she had been trying to find a nice woman to introduce him to. She said I would be the perfect woman for him. I asked her how well did she know him. She said she had been dating his brother for a couple of years and sometimes they would take him out with them because he didn't have anybody. She said they all went to the same church and they all grew up in that church. She said his father was a Deacon and his mother was on the Mothers Board, and they were raised in the church. She said he was a little older than me, but he was one of the good ones. I told her I guess it would be alright just to meet him. She was so happy. She said she would arrange the meeting. The next day at work she told me her boyfriends' birthday was coming up and she was going to give him a surprise birthday party. She said that would be the day she introduce us. The party was two weeks away. I told her that was fine with me, that would give me time to decide if I really wanted to do this. She asked me if it would be alright for her to tell him about me. I told her only after she tell me more about him. She told me he was her boyfriends' older brother. He was tall, dark and handsome. She said he had been married before and he has two sons, but they live with their mother. She said he was a good dresser. She said she didn't know what he did (job), but he was a nice guy who just needed to meet a nice woman. I said okay for her to tell him something about me. She was so excited this was going to happen. She was more excited about us than she was about planning the party. After the first week she said he wanted to get my telephone number so we could talk. I told her she could give it to him. She asked me not to try to see him before she got the chance to formally introduce us. I agreed. As soon as she gave him my number he called me that evening. He had a deep voice and it sounded good. He asked if we could meet before the party, but I told him I promised I would wait. He didn't press me any further. We talked for over an hour. He called me everyday and every time he called he asked if we could meet. A few days before the party he called and he told me he was going to be downtown and it would be so nice if I would let him come by. He said he wouldn't let our friend know that we met before the party. He said he wanted to introduce himself and he promised not to stay long because he was still at work. He said part of his job is out in the field, that is why he was coming downtown. I agreed to let him come by. Now I was nervous. One of the good features about my apartment was we had cameras in the lobby and you could view the lobby on your television and the person in the lobby would not know. I knew when he got there I would see him first and if I didn't like what I saw I did not have to answer my buzzer. When I heard my buzzer go off I immediately turned on my television. There he was, John #13, tall, dark and somewhat handsome. I buzzed him in. I made sure I was presentable and when I opened the door all he could say was "Wow". He came in and he said, "You are beautiful". I said, "Thank you handsome". He just stared at me, and I asked him to come in and have a seat. He said he was sorry he couldn't wait till the party to meet me. We laughed. He told me he sold Insurance and one of his clients was in the downtown area, so he was hoping I would let him come by. We chatted for a few minutes and then he had to leave. He said now he could wait for the party. I told him they would be picking me up because that is when we were going to be introduced. He said he wouldn't tell if I didn't tell. I agreed. No sooner than he had left the building, I called my girlfriend and told her we already met. I told her she was right, he is tall, dark and handsome. I thanked her for thinking of me. I told her I told him I wouldn't let you know we already met. I said we would play it off, so when they came to pick me up, we would both act surprised. The night of the party came and when they came to pick me up I wish I had a camera to capture the look on his face when I opened the door. His mouth fell wide open. I had on a dress that hugged my body and it had a fishtail in the back. It had shoulder pads which made my waist look even smaller. I had on black stockings with seams down the back of my legs. I had on 3 inch heels with straps that wrapped around my ankles. After they came in I closed the door and I had to go to my bedroom to get my purse, which meant he would get the view of the back of me. We were introduced and I met her boyfriend. He thought we were all going out together, he still didn't know about the party. The party was at their sister house, and he thought she was going out with us too. The party was nice and John #13 and I had a good time. After the party he took me home and we were married the following year. I was 30 and he was 40. I didn't marry him for the sex, it was only okay. I wanted to be someones wife, and I thought he would be a good husband to me. I moved from downtown. I thought this was it and he was the one. Well, it wasn't and he wasn't. The nice guy turned out to be a compulsive gambler, an all night rambler and a woman beater. I didn't find out until after we were married. He gambled so much, some nights and some weekends he wouldn't come home. Some days when I thought he was at work, he was at the race track. He wasn't a good gambler because he lost more than he won. Then he started stealing money from his job. He stole so much that he couldn't pay it back before it was discovered. They fired him. The first time he hit me he left his hand print on my face. He hit me so hard I actually saw stars. When he left for work the next day I changed the locks on the door so he couldn't get back in. A few days later my father passed. I did not want to go thru that alone. I was miserable. I contacted John #13 at his parents house. He promised me it wouldn't happen again, so I gave him another chance. Well the next time he tried to hold me down and beat me. When I saw him draw back his fist I screamed for our neighbors to call the police. I kicked and fought back till I could get up and I ran out of our apartment in my underwear. I ran down the hall yelling and sreaming asking for someone to call the police. That was the last time we shared any space together. To make matters worse he even found the time to cheat on me. I thought since I was 10 years younger than him I wouldn't have to worry. Not true. I divorced John #13 after almost only two years of marriage. The bad days greatly out weighed the good days. I thought about Jerome. I never remember a time when he got mad at me. Not even when I left for college. He was sad about me leaving, but he was not mad at me. He was always kind to me. I wondered how he was doing. I moved out of the apartment.

Chapter 21

My girlfriend felt so bad that she had introduced me to John #13. She and her husband, which was his brother that she married, kept apologizing to me everytime they saw me. I had to tell them to stop apologizing because they were not responsible for his actions. They must have felt it was their duty to find me someone else who could erase all that pain for me and them. Her husband decided he wanted me to meet one of his friends that he worked with. My girlfriend also agreed. I asked them to tell me about him. They looked at each other like they didn't know what to say. My girlfriend told me how handsome he was and how much of a gentleman he was. She said he was her husband best friend. He was very reliable. Her husband filled in the information she hadn't told me. He was married. He and his wife lived their own lives and he was sure his wife was cheating on him. He said his friend had talked about getting a divorce. At this point I had my own conversation in my head. I told myself I have not had any luck with all the single men that I had dated, maybe a married man is what I needed. If there is no commitment maybe he will act right. We won't see each other every day, maybe it will make our time together more meaningful. He can't cheat on me because he is cheating with me. Maybe I should give this a try. I can't lose him, he's not mine. I never thought I would do anything like this. I told them I was willing to meet him to see if we liked each other. We met and she was right, he was very handsome. He knew I had already been informed about his situation. He told me he would be very discreet and he would appreciate any time that I spent with him. He was John #14. We started meeting in the mornings before I went to work. He would be getting off work when I was going to work. I had gotten a car at this time. I would get in his car and we would find a secluded place to park. We would sit in his car and talk, kiss and fool around. I remember we met one evening and we went for a drive. We drove to a park and we got out and sat under the stars and laughed and talked as we cuddled together under a tree. Things started changing. He wanted to get intimate. I did too. He took a day off work, but his wife did not know, and he came over. We laughed and talked. But this time we had sex. He was an older guy and he made love like an older guy. I wanted more but he didn't have more to give me. I layed there feeling unfulfilled. He was happy, but I was flustered. I thought maybe he was just nervous since this was our first time and it will get better. It didn't get any better. John #14 was very handsome, but he wasn't much in bed. We still met in the mornings and he started making requests. He asked me to jerk him off in the car. That turned into our daily habit. I would give him a hand job and he would go home smiling. I had another conversation with myself. I remembered how I felt when I found out my husband was cheating on me. I remembered the pain and betrayal I felt. I remember wanting to hurt the woman and my husband. I asked myself how could I do the same thing to this woman that those other women and my husband did to me. I said I didn't deserve that and she don't deserve this. My mother did not raise me that way. My mother would be so disappointed with me if she knew what I was doing. Whatever problem he and his wife are having, he is just going to have to suck it up and work it out. The next time John #14 came over I told him I couldn't do this anymore. I told him my conscience won't let me. I told him my husband cheated on me and I am no better than him if I continue to do this. I had to stop. John #14 said he understood and he really appreciated all the times we spent together. He said I made him feel good and he would always be thankful for that. I told myself it didn't matter if he understood or not, this was going to stop. We didn't have sex that day. After our conversation was over, he left. I could tell he was very sad, but I felt better about myself. I told myself I cannot become someone that I can't face in the morning. I will never sink that low again. I don't care if I never meet another man. I don't want someone else man, I want my own. Thoughts of Jerome crossed my mind. I would like to know where he is. I really wanted to see him.

Chapter 22

I guess this must have been the time that all my fiends thought they had the perfect guy for me. They all wanted to introduce me to someone. I didn't make it any better, because I let them. Another one of my friends wanted me to meet one of her friends. She and I worked together and we lived in the same apartment building. She invited me down to her apartment and introduced me to several of her friends. I got the attention of one of them and he said he would like to talk to me. We talked for a minute and then I said I had to go. Her friend asked me if he could call me because he would really like to see me again. He seemed like a nice guy so I gave him my telephone humber. This was John #15. He called me later that night and we talked for a while. He asked if he could come over and I told him he could come over on the weekend because I had some things I had to do. He agreed. The weekend came and John #15 came over. He didn't stop at his friend apartment downstairs, he came straight up to mine. When I moved after my divorce I had gotten rid of most of the furniture, so I only had my bedroom furniture and my dinette set. When John #15 came in I told him we would have to sit at the table. He said he would like to sit on the floor. I rolled the television into the living room and we sat on the floor. This was our get acquainted date. We had pleasant conversation. He was not married and he didn't have any kids. He occasionally went to church. He had a job, but I can't remember what it was. I was listening but not really hearing. He also drank and smoked. I knew that was going to be a problem for me, but I was willing to give it a try. His first visit lasted a couple hours. When he left he told me he was going to stop by his friend apartment downstairs just to say "Hi". I figured he was going to tell her how things went with us. I needed to know if he was a 'kiss and tell' kind of guy. But before I could finish my thoughts he told me he did not discuss his personal business with his friends. He said they may laugh and talk and drink together, but he don't share his business. I wanted to believe him, but I said time will tell. We talked on the phone all week and he came over the following weekend. This time he brought dinner with him. We sat at the table and ate and then we sat on the floor in front of the television. This time we sat closer and we kissed. It was a good kiss, so he gave me another one. I got up because I wanted to slow things down. I didn't want him to think just because he brought me dinner he was entitled to some sexual pleasure. He knew why I got up. He said he couldn't help himself, he wanted to kiss me the first day he met me. He said he would leave because he could feel it was getting tense and he didn't want me to be uncomfortable in my own apartment. He left and he did not stop at his friend apartment. He called me the next day to see if we were still alright. I told him I appreciate what he did and everything was fine. He told me he can't make excuses for being a man, and he found me to be very desirable. John #15 was turning out to be a good guy. We got together the next weekend. This time when things got hot we both went with the flow. The sex was good, but afterwards he lit a cigarette and that kind of blew it for me. He knew I didn't smoke so he opened the window and stood in front of it as he smoked. We had sex again, and again. It was good. He fell asleep after wards. I let him sleep for a while. Althought I enjoyed the sex, something just didn't feel right. I looked at him while he was sleeping and I remember thinking, "What are you doing Anita, he is not the one." I knew I needed more than sex from a man and I couldn't see myself with him in the future. That was a strange thought, but I felt my interest in him drop. I woke him up and we showered and got dressed. He gave me a long passionate kiss and he left. I don't know what I was feeling, but it wasn't good. After that night I think I saw him one more time and when he came over he brought a bottle of liquor with him. I knew at that point it was not going to work. We didn't see each other anymore. I think he knew it too. I don't even remember who stopped calling who. It was a nice ride, but I had to get off. I moved out of the building. I didn't want to live around anyone that I worked with anymore. I didn't want my business to be the subject of discussion at work. I was searching for something, but I had no idea what it was.

Chapter 23

I was enjoying my new apartment. It was a few blocks from my mothers house. I could walk to her house anytime I wanted to see her. I was still going to church. I was doing fine by myself. The church picnic was coming up. Several times at church I noticed one of the members kept watching me. When I would look at him he would quickly turn his head like he wasn't looking at me. When he walked by me he would smile and speak to me, but only to say "Good morning." I thought that was funny because he was always watching me. I figured he would find the nerve one day to say more. The day of the church picnic came and I guess he found the nerve because he walked up to me and asked me if he could talk to me. I said, "Sure we can talk." He asked if we could walk around the park as we talked and I agreed. He told me he had been wanting to talk to me for a long time. He said he kept putting it off and then it was too late because I married John #13. He said he was a long time friend of that family. Then he said he didn't think it would be right if he started talking to me right after I had divorced him. But now he said he told himself he had better say something before someone else try to talk to me. He asked if it would be okay for him to call me. I told him that would be fine, so I gave him my telephone number. We walked and talked for a long time. This was John #16. Everyone had a good time at the picnic. Me, John #13 and John #16 were all members of the same church. John #13 stopped coming to church after we divorced. John #16 came to church all the time. We started dating. He would come over to visit me and I wondered when he would invite me to his place. I would invite him over for dinner and he would take me out to dinner. When John

#13 found out that we were dating he thought he could stop us by asking me to come back to him. He thought he could intimidate John #16 because he was much bigger than him, and he would stop seeing me. But it didn't work, so he just faded out of the picture. We had been seeing each other for a while and I knew sex would be coming up soon. And it did. We were at my apartment watching a movie and we were all hugged up sitting on the couch. I turned my head to look at him and he gave me a long awaited kiss. It was long and passionate. One kiss lead to another and then another. We were soon taking off our clothes and we had sex right there on the couch. It was wonderful. I could tell he had been waiting for that moment, and I realized I had been waiting for it too. It was not a quickly, we went at it for about an hour. He really knew what to do! It was kind of awkward after it was over, because we didn't know what to say. I think we both were sexually frustrated. We cleaned up and got dressed. He gave me another long kiss and he left. I enjoyed the sex very much, but something was bothering me and I didn't know what it was. We kept seeing each other. I went to visit him at his place and I learned that John #16 liked to drink beer. He liked it a lot. He would drink until he got sloppy drunk. In my mind a red flag went up, but I ignored it. I liked him and the sex was great. I met some of his friends and they drank just as much as he did. He was living two different lives. He had his church life and he had his street life. He kept the two lives separate, and he did a good job concealing one from the other until he met me. I didn't know that not only was he living two lives, but he had a woman for each life. I was his church woman and he had another woman for his street life. She and I bumped heads when I popped up at his place one day. It was an ugly scene. She saw me and she got really mad with him and started cussing him out. He got in between us and pushed me into another room and shut the door so she could not see me. I heard them yelling and cussing at each other. He told her she had better not say anything to me. He told her whatever she had to say she had to say it to him. He told her whatever happens at this point was his fault. She asked him to open the door so she could see me and he told her that was not going to happen. I was on the other side of the door ready to throw down if it came to that. She was so mad she left and told him she was thru with him, and; she would not be back. He said he didn't care. After she left and he calmed down he opened the door of the room I was in and he apologized to me. He said he did not want me to see this side of him.

I realized that was not the life I wanted to live. He said if I had not come over that day he don't know if and when he would have ever told me. He said he was not going to be seeing her anymore. But I wondered to myself if that only meant he was going to find another woman to take her place. Sunday morning came and John #16, the church man, was all dressed up looking and smelling good. I looked at him and I had to shake my head. He was going to continue playing the role and living two different lives. Then one day something happened that shook my whole world. The two lives collided. John #16 came over and I just was not feeling him that day. Something didn't feel right. I was sensing something sinister was about to happen. He wanted to have sex but I didn't. He kept trying to get me to give in. I kept saying I didn't want to do it. We got into a wrestling match. I couldn't believe he was trying to force me to do something I said I didn't want to do. Then he managed to pin me down on the couch. He had his knees on my arms and I couldn't move. I couldn't believe what was happening. I kept telling him to get off me, but he was determined he was going to get what he wanted. I was so shocked and hurt that he was doing this to me, I guess I went into shock because I stopped resisting and I froze. I guess he thought I stopped because I was in agreement. He proceeded to have sex with me, and it didn't make any difference to him that I was not responding. He forced himself inside of me. He actually raped me. When he finished he looked down at me, still not responding, and he said, "You made me fight for that one." I still was not responding. He went and cleaned up and left. I was still laying on the couch when he left. It was maybe 20 minutes or more before I started moving. When I sat up I cried. I couldn't believe what had happened. I felt so violated and so disappointed. He called me the next day and I told him if he ever touched me again one of us was surely going to die. He acted like he couldn't understand whay I was so angry. I didn't tell anyone what had happened. The next time I saw him at church he could tell it was best that he not speak to me or come near me. He continued living that double life. It worked for him, but it didn't work for me. I tried, but after what happened, I saw too much of the street life that I could not deal with. He was not the man for me and I knew it.

Chapter 24

I walked to my mothers house one day and when I got there she was sitting on the porch. I loved to sit on the porch with my mother. My sister was there too. They told me about one of their new neighbors. They said he was a real nice guy. He had two kids and they were all really friendly people. They said he was a good cook. He had barbecued one day and brought them some of his food and they said it was really good. I knew if my mother ate it, it had to be good because my mother did not eat everyones cooking. They told me his name and I told them he was a member of my church. While I was sitting on the porch he came outside. When we saw each other he came over to the porch and we greeted each other with a hug and a kiss on the cheek. He was surprised that was my mother and sister. We all laughed. I didn't know his kids, but I knew his mother, father and some of his siblings. From that day on every time I came over to my mothers house he would come outside. He lived across the street. I would go over to his house and sit on the porch with him too. We talked a lot. He did most of the talking. He truly had the gift of gab. He became John #17. Sometimes he would walk down to my apartment to visit me. He had been gone from church for a while. He was on some kind of minister assignment at another church. I forgot to mention he was a preacher. But he was ready to come back to his home church. We would see each other at church when he came. A couple of times he rode to church with me. We started spending a lot of time together. The kiss on the cheek moved to the lips. The friendly hug became a romantic embrace. He was inviting me to dinner and I was inviting him to dinner.

We would watch movies at my apartment and I would watch movies at his house. One of his kids was a teenager and she looked out for her little brother. They were both well mannered kids. When John #17 was at my place my mother and sister kept an eye on his kids. I guess he had been coming over for a while and this day he came over he let it be known to me that he wanted more than just a hug and kiss. So we wound up in bed in the middle of the afternoon. I can only describe what we did as scary. He was very aggressive and he made a lot of loud grunting sounds. He was trying to be dominating, but he came across as trying too hard. He was trying to do everything he knew how to do to please me, but it wasn't enough. I said to myself, when this is over it will never happen again. I think he knew it was not good. After it was over he said it should not have happened, and I agreed. We both agreed to just be friends because sex would only complicate things. We became better friends. When I would go visit my mother he would come out and speak to me and go back in the house. If he didn't come out and speak to me I would go and knock on his door and speak to him. We never mentioned what had happened in my apartment. I must admit that was one of the worst sexual experiences I had ever had. But then I remembered John #7. I don't know why I allowed this to happen. There was no real chemistry. I think he was just convenient because he was in the neighborhood. Whatever it was that I was looking for, I definitely did not find it. I told myself I would never do anything for convenience sake again. I moved from my apartment because I wanted to be closer to my church. John #17 moved shortly after I did. I didn't stop sitting on the porch with my mother. I would still come over and sit with her. Sometimes I would fix us some coffee and we would sit on the porch and drink our coffee. I really miss those days.

Chapter 25

I was a very active member of my church. I was an Usher, I sang in one of the Choirs, and I was a Sunday School Teacher. I did well in church but I was a flop in romance. I just couldn't seem to get with the right man. I told myself I was going to stop trying and just focus on my duties in the church. I was happy and doing fine. It was my Sunday to Usher and while I was standing at the door a man approached me and introduced himself to me. He was a member of the church, but he had been away for a while. He told me I must be a new member because he don't remember seeing me before. I found out he had been gone from the church due to his job. We talked for a moment and then I ushered him to a seat. He asked if we could talk after service. I said it would be alright. He was a tall dark handsome man with a bright smile. After service he came directly to me and asked if he could take me out to eat. I said yes. I told him I could meet him at the restaurant because I had my own car. I could tell he wanted me to ride with him. He drove a Cadillac. We had just met and I didn't know him, and I didn't want to get in his car. He told me to follow him, and I did. When we got to the restaurant he asked me if I was nervous about being in the car with him since we just met. I told him I just like to be cautious. He said he understood. We had an afternoon service so we had about two hours to eat. Dinner and the conversation were fine. He told me a lot about himself. He had a couple of jobs and one of them was as a Dejay on the Radio. He had the perfect voice for Radio, it was deep and piercing. Dinner was over and we headed back to church. He told me he enjoyed dinner with me and he would like to see me again. We exchanged telephone numbers.

We talked a lot on the telephone and he came over several times. This was John #18. We were getting closer. I liked him and I knew he liked me. A couple of months had gone by and the only romantic gesture he had made was kissing. Then one night when he came over the kiss advanced into sex. It was alright. He had a trick or two. He spent the night and he asked me to come with him the next morning while he did his spot on the Radio. I was excited about going to see him while he was talking on the Radio. He did not tell me his show started at 6:00 a.m., which meant we had to get up at about 4:00 a.m. to be there on time. I was still excited about going, but I was not excited about getting up so early. I watched him as he got everything ready. He made coffee and there were snacks. He sat in the booth and I sat in an adjoining both watching him. It was time to go on the air. It was a Gospel Station. I was so excited, you would have thought I was going on the air. He sounded good on the radio. People were up and tuned in when he went on. His callers would make song requests and he would play their songs and announce their name over the air. He asked me what song I would like to hear. While the song was playing he had a button he would hit so we could talk while the record was playing. When he played my song he announced my name on the air. I felt like a groupie. His show was from 6:00-12:00. He asked me to help him find the songs that people were requesting. I felt like I was on the radio too. I was really impressed. This was a good date. I had never done anything like that before. After the show was over we went to get something to eat. I thought I would be sleepy and want to go back home and get back in the bed, but I wasn't. After we ate he took me home. I was really turned on from watching him work. We had sex again. Afterwards he cleaned up, got dressed and left. He had to get to his other job. I thought this was going to be a good relationship. As time went on I was beginning to see what I thought was charm, was cocky. He was the type of person you couldn't tell him anything because he knew it all. If I gave my opinion about something, he would tell me I was wrong and proceed to tell me what I should have said. He had an annoying habit of always tapping me when he talked, and it was driving me crazy. I also noticed that he talked a lot, sometimes too much. I must not had been paying attention when we first met, because he was very opinionated, and he could never see anyone else view. I didn't like it. He made me wish he had never introduced himself to me. I weighed my options. He was not the man I thought I wanted. I had to get away from him and do it quick. I just stopped answering his calls. Whoever invented Caller Id, was a genius. He eventually got the message and we stopped seeing each other.

Chapter 26

I guess I was really on a roll for attracting the wrong man. Valentines Day was coming up and one Sunday at church one of our preachers walked by me while I was sitting down waiting for service to start and dropped a card in my lap. It was in a red envelope so I knew it was a Valentine Card. I was surprised because we had never had a conversation. I opened the card and read it. It stated that he would like to be my Valentine, and he also wrote his telephone number on the card. I laughed. I'm sure he was expecting a reply from me, but when service was over I left without saying a word to him. I hoped his attempt to get my attention was over. I wasn't trying to hook up with anyone. I was thinking about all the disappointing relationships I had and the picture didn't look good. How could I make so many mistakes. I thought I was following my heart. Something wasn't clicking. Maybe I was over looking something or was I seeing something that wasn't really there. I told myself love couldn't be this complicated. My birthday was coming up and this preacher gave me a beautiful Birthday Card. I didn't know what to think. I felt I could at least thank him for the card. I did. There was going to be an Ordination Service at our church, It would be for 3 Deacons and 1 Preacher, and he was the preacher to be ordained. I had never witnessed an Odination and I was curious about it. I was told the candidates had to answer a series of questions to determine if they were worthy of their office in the church. If they failed to answer the questions they would not be allowed to hold their positions. If they passed they would be given papers and installed into their positions. The day of the Ordination came and all the candidates did well. After the service I went up to congratulate each one of them and he asked me not to leave until he had a chance to talk to me. I waited for him. He asked me out for dinner to celebrate with him and a couple of his friends. I knew them too. We all had a good time laughing and talking. He asked if he could call me and since I was having a good time, I gave him my telephone number. He called me daily and to my surprise I enjoyed his conversations. He was a few years younger than me. I remembered the last younger guy that I dated didn't work out so well. I didn't want to judge him by what the other guy did. We went out to dinner, just the two of us and I could tell this guy liked me. He was John #19. After dinner we went back to his house. As soon as I stepped inside the door he grabbed me and kissed me. He said he had been waiting for months to do that. We talked for a while and then he took me home. I wasn't sure about this relationship because he was a preacher and I knew there had to be some guidelines. I thought! It was about a month later when we had sex. It just happened one night at his house. I was leery about doing it, but in the heat of passion we both gave in. It was good. I was afraid we both would be struck down by lightening for giving in to our flesh. The preachers world was new to me. I thought they had some kind of rules that they had to follow. When I told him what I thought, he laughed. He told me he is still a man with needs and desires. He said we are consenting adults and a preacher should be looking for a wife and not a girlfriend. I didn't know how to take that comment. As time went on he got invited to different churches to go and preach. I would go with him to support him. Many times the people at the other churches thought I was his wife. I supported him a lot and we made a handsome couple. I remember our first Christmas together. I wanted to get him something special. One day while at work I went out at lunch time to a famous hat store to buy him a hat with matching gloves. On my way back to work I slipped and fell and I broke my ankle. I was immediately taken to the hospital. I called him to let him know what had happened and he came and got me and took me home. I had given the present that I bought for him to one of my friends that was with me when I fell. I told her to keep it until I called for it because I didn't want him to see it. I was off work for two months. I gave him his gift on Christmas and I was expecting to get a ring, but I got perfume instead. I was disappointed. He saw the look on my face when I opened my gift, but he didn't say anything. I said to myself, I don't hink we are on the same page. I never told him what I was expecting to happen and he never explained. We continued to date, but I was starting to feel like something wasn't right. I wasn't feeling fulfilled anymore, something had changed. I don't know if it was me or him. Everything started feeling wrong. I couldn't explain it. It was my birthday again and I had not heard from him all day. I called him a couple of times while I was at work and I got no answer. When I got home I checked my answering machine and there were no messages from him. This was not like him to go all day without calling me. Night time came and still no word from him. I went to his house and thru the window I could see he was home. I rung the doorbell. He didn't answer. I Knocked on the door, but he didn't answer. I stood back and looked toward the window and I could see his shadow moving around in the house. I knocked again. Still no answer. I stood on the porch trying to figure out what was going on. The next thing that happened really blew me away. While I was standing on the porch the police pulled up and got out of their car. They came on the porch and asked me who I was, and then they asked to see my ID. I told them who I was and I showed them my ID. They said they received a report that an unwanted person was at this house banging on the door. The owner of the house wanted this person removed from their property. My mouth fell open. They asked me what was my relationship with the home owner, and I told them we were dating. They asked if we had had a disagreement. I told them we had not had any kind of disagreement. I told them it was my birthday and we were suppose to be getting together. They saw my birthdate on my license. They told me they had to respond to the complaint, and maybe he had some issues going on that I didn't know about. They said they had to ask me to leave, and I should give him some time to work out whatever the problem might be. I was so embarrassed because all of his neighbors were looking. Needless to say that relationship was over. I asked myself how could someone who says they love me treat me like this. I was angry and hurt. This could not be real love. I was totally blind sided and it took me a while to get over that.

Chapter 27

People are the same everywhere. Some people think they are the perfect match makers. One of the members at my church thought it would be a good idea for me to meet her brother. She said I was a good and kind woman and that was the kind of woman that her brother needed. She introduced us one day at church. We talked for a few minutes and he asked if he could call me. I gave him my telephone number. He called a couple days later. We talked and learned more about each other. He told me a lot about his past and I told him about mine. He was living in a half way house with several other guys and they had rules that they had to follow. I didn't know much about half way houses. He was also taking a class at a local college. I went to visit him one day and I met everyone in the house. They were all friendly guys. We talked on a daily basis. He was a nice guy who got caught up in the drug scene and now he was trying to get his life back on track. I didn't know anything about drugs. He was the first person that I had met that had any drug experience. When I visited him we would watch movies together with the other guys. I wanted him to come to my place so we could be alone. There were rules he had to follow whenever he left, and he also had household duties that had to be done before he could go anywhere. I picked him up one day and we went back to my apartment. We picked up some food and some movies. We enjoyed out time together. We enjoyed it so much that we began kissing and it led to having sex. It was very good. We both were out of breath when we stopped. When I took him back home we were both grinning from ear to ear. We kissed and he went inside. He was John #20. On Sundays his sister would pick him up for church. I was visiting him more often. He was inviting me to accompany him to his family functions. We were enjoying each others company. I asked him if he wanted to move out of the half way house. He told me he just needed to have some place to move, and he would be responsible for his soveriety. I let him move in with me. He moved in, but he would not sleep with me. He slept on the floor and sometimes on the couch. I didn't understand that action. He said he didn't want to feel like he only moved in so we could have sex all the time. He said he still had to fight every day to stay clean, and he needed to stay focused. We only had sex that one time. He was attending a class weekly and he was also a musician. He played the guitar. He played the guitar at church when the choirs sang. It wasn't long when I noticed that his behavior was changing. He seemed to be very irritable. I noticed one day when he came in that he did not have his guitar. I asked him about it and he said he was at a friends house rehearsing a song and he left it over there with his friend. I didn't think anything was wrong about that. Another day he came in and he was very upset. He said he had a confrontation with someone in the class. I didn't see anything wrong with that either. Then another day he said he needed a few dollars to get his guitar out of the pawn shop. This was the guitar he said he left at a friends house. He said he had to pawn it to have money for a book he needed to buy for the class. That didn't sound right to me, but I didn't say anything. Then his family members started calling and asking me were we alright, moneywise, because John #20 was also borrowing money from them. Then I knew what was wrong. He was back on drugs. I knew he had to go. His family confronted him and he admitted he had fallen. He apologized to me and them and said he wanted to go back to the half way house if they would let him come back. They did let him come back. We still called each other and he continued coming to church. It was only a few weeks when I noticed a female member at church started paying a lot of attention to him. I would see her walk by him and say something to him. She did it everytime she saw him. Then one day I saw her slip him a piece of paper. John #20 and I was talking everyday until she gave him that piece of paper, which was probably her telephone number. Now we were talking maybe two or three times a week. Then it dropped to once a week. When I would see him at church I couldn't get a full conversation with him because he would be over in a corner talking to the other woman. I asked him what was going on and he told me she was just someone that he had gone to school with and there was nothing going on. I discovered that was a lie. She was now visiting him at the half way house and he was visiting her. I was angry at first, but I got over it. I said they deserve each other and whatever happens. I asked myself why do grown ups feel they have to lie about what they want. If you don't want me and you want some one else just say so. That will not kill me, I will survive and press on. I thought about Jerome and I wondered where he was. I knew when we were dating he only wanted me. I wanted a man who could feel about me the way Jerome did.

Chapter 28

Romance was not working for me. I just couldn't seem to meet the right guy. I wondered how many men would I have to meet before I found the right man for me. One of my girlfriends felt I needed something else to focus on. Something that would take my mind off my troubles for a while. She invited me to go to a convention with her. It was an Amway Convention. I said what the heck, it is something different to do. I went with her. It was very festive and exciting. I met a lot of people. I had no intentions of joining. I just went because she was my friend. She introduced me to a group of people that was a part of her team. She had men and women, young and old on her team. I wound up going to her next meeting and I joined. I bought my kit and I made my list of people that I was going to show the plan. I noticed each time one of our team members had a meeting the team would show up in support. We started becoming a family. However, there was one male team member that I thought was very handsome. He was a few years younger than me and we kidded around a lot with each other. When there was a convention out of town, I would go with my girlfriend, her husband and this man. Our kidding around started getting personal. It was almost a year before we took it to the bedroom. Yes, he was John #21. We both knew we should not have done it, but we got caught up in the heat of passion. We thought we could be just sex buddies with no strings attached. It sounded good to me. My girlfriend told me that our group leader did not encourage any kind of personal relationships between team members. We felt we could keep our personal relationship on the down low. We continued to have sex. He would come to my apartment and I would go to his house. The sex wasn't the best, but it took the edge off when things weren't going to good. The sex was going better than I was at getting people on my team. I knew I was not cut out to do Amway but I kept trying. I went to all the conventions that they had. I had the chance to travel, which I never would have done if I had not joined. I met tons of people. Eventually John #21 and I stopped having sex. We remained friends. I realized I was not the sex buddy type of woman. I couldn't just have casual sex. My heart goes with my vagina. What was I thinking. I needed to find Mr. Right, or Mr. Right needed to find me right away. I also realized Amway was not for me. I didn't like selling. I didn't like hosting meetings, and I did not need to constantly buy products because it was only me. I stopped going to the meetings. I stopped selling and I stopped buying. John #21 was doing better than me in the business. He had several people on his team. I supported my girlfriend when I could. I stopped going around our group. This was suppose to take my mind off my problems with romance, but instead it only made me think about it more. I said to myself, if I had the right man we could run this business together and really be successful.

Chapter 29

I was so frustrated with romance. I didn't feel like I would ever find Mr. Right. The one thing that I knew that was right for me was my relationship with the Lord. I decided I would put all my energy on strengthening my relationship with the Lord. I knew the Lord loved me and no one could take that from me. Then one night at Bible Class I met John #22. Our pastor was giving us an open book quiz. He would quote part of a scripture and we had to find it in the Bible and give the complete scripture. John #22 was sitting in front of me and he would keep turning around and try to give me the answer. I told him I could find the scripture by myself. A couple of times I found it before he did. After class he came up to me and introduced himself. He asked me how long had I been studying because I really seemed to know the Bible. We talked for a few minutes and he said he was looking for a Bible Study Partner. He asked if I had a study partner. I told him I studied by myself. He asked if I would like to be his partner. I told him I would have to think about it. He said that would be fine and I could let him know what I decided. We were both active members in the church. I had been a member longer than him. He was a Deacon. It was Sunday morning and he approached me when I got to the church and asked if I had thought about what he asked me. I told him I would let him know my answer at Bible Class on Wednesday. He said that was good enough. I wasn't sure that I wanted to study with him. I thought about it during service. I watched him during service and he seemed to be a dedicated Deacon who loved the Word of God. Wednesday night at Bible Class I told him we could be study partners. He was happy with my decision. I figured I could learn from him. After class he asked me to come by his house so we could set up our study plan. I was impressed that he wanted to get started right away. He lived only a few blocks from the church, so I followed him home in my car. When I went inside I met his daughter, she lived with him. We decided we would study the Sunday School Lessons and any Bible Class assignments the pastor gave us. We set up the time and the day that we would come together. We would meet once a week. The first study session was going to be at my apartment. The day he came over I had prepared some light snacks. Before we got started he read a scripture, I sang a song and he said a prayer. This was our weekly routine. We would study the Sunday School Lesson and take turns reading it out loud. Then we would discuss what we read and answer the study questions at the end of the lesson. If we had an assignment from Bible Class we would meet twice a week. Everything was going well. John #22 was always so kind and thoughtful. He was being a real gentleman. We also learned a lot about each other during our sessions. He was divorced, had six children, both of his parents and his two brothers were all deceased, and he was a former drug addict. He said the Lord delivered him from drugs and he was so grateful. He said he took life one day at a time and he took nothing for granted. I was concerned about the drug issue. I asked him how long had he been clean and he said for a couple of years. He asked if we could always meet at my apartment for our study sessions because his house was always busy. I agreed. Each time we met we shared more about ourselves. He told me about the church he went to before he came to our church. He said his former pastor helped him to get clean and he would always be thankful to him for that. We had been studying together for several months before things started to change. One night after we had finished studying John #22 said he needed to tell me something. I immediately thought he was going to tell me he was back on drugs. I was holding my breath. He told me he was interested in me and not just as a study partner, he said for romance. I was relieved it wasn't about drugs, but I didn't know what to say. I had other thoughts about him too. We kissed and one thing led to another and before I knew it we were in my bed. The sex was great and it was over an hour before we stopped. We began dating. During the course of our dating John #22 announced that the Lord had called him into the ministry. He discussed it with our pastor and he was accepted into the ministry. I remember his first sermon. It was a powerful message. Our relationship got really intensed. I really cared about him and I was helping him hide a big secret from everybody, including his family. The secret was that John #22 had started using drugs again. I didn't want anyone to be looking down on him, so everytime he would get high I would clean him up. I would make sure he was presentable on Sunday morning. I thought I was helping him, but now I realize I was encouraging him to keep getting high. I gave him my word I would support him and never leave him, and he held me to my word. We got married and I was still keeping the secret. During our marriage my mother passed and John #22 conducted the funeral. No one knew about all the fights we had prior to and leading up to my mothers funeral. My husband was actually jealous of the fact that I didn't have to make the funeral arrangements by myself, because I had siblings and we helped and comforted each other. When his mother passed he had to do everything by himself. I couldn't grieve for my mother because I had to deal with his drug problem. On the day of my mothers funeral I found out that my best friend died, and she was like a sister to me. I couldn't grieve for her either because of his drug problem. He got high the day after my mothers funeral. I was really unhappy. His sometime drug use escalated into everyday drug use. It got to the point of him starting to get violent toward me. I knew I could not keep this secret any longer because he had also started threatening me with a gun. I told our pastor and I prayed for the Lord to get me out of that situation before he killed me. Not only was he getting high, but he was also cheating on me with several women and some of them were prostitutes. The Lord delivered me from that dangerous situation. I moved out of the house after six years and filled for a divorce. We were married eight years by the time the divorce was granted. It was not easy putting that nightmare behind me. I had so much anger and hurt bottled up inside me, I had to find a release. I wrote a book about my marriage and that was my way of releasing everything that I was feeling. Now I was ready to move on. The title of my book is "Memoirs of a Preachers Wife, Things Only God Knew". Needless to say John #22 wasn't happy, when my book came out. He couldn't argue with the truth.

Chapter 30

I had bought a Laptop Computer when I wrote my book, because I needed to submit my book to the publisher online. I don't remember how I got on Face book, but I found out I could communicate with people I had not seen in a long time. I connected with schoolmates and relatives. This was a very useful tool. I thought about Jerome. I said he is the only person from my past that I would really like to see again. I didn't know how to find him, so I asked someone on Facebook how do you contact people. She told me how to search for someone. I put his name in search, but I didn't get anything. I was disappointed. My friend told me that could mean he might not be on Facebook, but I could keep trying because one day he may be on it. This was the beginning of my search for Jerome. A year had gone by and I had not dated anyone. I wasn't interested in dating because I didn't trust anyone and I didn't trust my own judgement about men. One day at work as I was coming in the building one of the security guards met me at the door and he told me that he thought I was a very beautiful woman. I smiled at him and walked away. I knew he was watching me walk away so I slowly strutted down the hall. The same security guard was at the door at the end of the day. He asked me if I would tell him my name. I smiled and told him my name. He smiled and said "Good night Miss Anita." Everyday he would give me a compliment. This went on for several weeks. Then one day as I was leaving he asked if he could speak to me for a minute. I let him speak. He told me he had been watching me for weeks and he would really like to get to know me. He quickly told me a little about himself. The one thing that stuck in my head was that he was

30 years old. I told him I was 52 and he looked surprised when I said it. He said he thought I was about 40. I smiled and asked him if he thought I might be too old for him. He said, "No Miss Anita, the way I see it is we are both adults." He gave me his telephone number and he asked if he could have mine. I took a deep breath and I gave it to him. I wasn't sure about this, but he was a handsome much younger man. Of course I was flattered and curious. The weekend was coming and he asked if he could take me out to dinner. I said yes. I gave him my address. He was John #23. We went to a Chinese Restaurant and we talked and told a little more about ourselves. I found out that he lived not too far from my mother. He was not from Highland Park, but he knew a lot of people in Highland Park. When I told him that I grew up in Highland Park he was surprised. I didn't know then, but I later found out he did not think anyone from Highland Park was worth anything. To be exact, his words were "worth shit". After dinner we went back to my apartment. We watched a movie and we got cozy. We started kissing and it led us to having sex on the couch. It was amazing. This much younger man knew how to do the do. I told him I did not intend for that to happen, but he said he was glad it did. As the weeks went by I learned more and more about him. The things I was learning were not good. We were on different pages in our thinking. He referred to women as "bitches". I told him I found that to be very disrespectful, but he told me he was not including me. I told him he was including all women, even his own mother and sister. He didn't see it that way. He also felt if a woman had three kids and they all had different fathers, she was a whore. I asked him what about the man who dated the woman with three kids and he still wanted to have sex with her, what does that say about him. His reply was, it is her responsibility to prevent another pregnancy, because a man is going to be a man and want sex. I could not believe his whole thought process. He liked that Gangster Rap Music, which I hate. I realized we were from two different planets and the generation gap was too big to close. We were not going to see eye to eye on very many things. I asked him what attracted him to me. He said he liked my style. He said he found my confidence very sexy. He said he enjoyed watching me walk, he said I had a powerful stroll. I was impressed with his answer. But I knew this was not going to work. I asked him what were his plans for his life, and he didn't have an answer. John #23 was not the man for me. We

met one afternoon and I told him we could not see each other anymore because we didn't really have anything in common outside of the bedroom, and that was not enough for me. At the same time our company changed their security service due to a serious problem with one of their security employees. This meant he was no longer going to be around. I never saw or heard from him again.

Chapter 31

I was at the shop getting my hair done and this guy came in selling some stuff. My hairdresser said this guy came in all the time and everyone in the shop knew him. He told me he was a nice guy. I can't remember what he was selling that day, but when he came over to my hairdresser, my hairdresser told him about my book and he asked him to buy a copy. He did. When he gave me his money he also asked me to write my telephone number in the book so he could call me when he needed more copies. I said to myself he is trying to be slick, but I played along with him and wrote my number under my autograph. He hung out at the shop longer than usual that day. He spent all of his time talking to me. He told me where he lived, where he worked, he was divorced, how many kids he had, and he said he took his mother out to dinner every Sunday. I thought this was a good man. He called me the next day, not for books, just to talk. I told him a little about me. He came over and he took me out to eat. He asked me if I liked jewelry. I said yes, and he went out to his car and he brought in a big bag full of all kinds of jewelry. He told me I could pick whatever I liked and I could have it. I picked a necklace set. He asked me if I had ever sold anything. I told him I used to be an Avon lady many years ago. I told him I worked with a lot of women and they would love to buy the jewelry he had. He asked me if I would take his bag to work with me and sell to my co-workers. He said he would split the money with me 50/50. I told him I would just like to see if I could do it and he wouldn't have to split the money with me. He said I could have whatever jewelry I wanted. I took his bag to work and sold everything I had. I sold almost $600. I called him and told him he needed to get more jewelry and I told him the kind of jewelry my co-workers liked. He was John #24. We were business partners as well. He got watches (men and women), more necklace sets and earrings (all sizes). From that bag I sold over $400. In between the selling we went out a few times, he was a lot of fun. The night we decided to get intimate was a real shocker. We was kissing and as we started to undress he kept saying, "Don't hurt my feelings". I thought he was talking about don't break his heart and leave him. I found out that was not what he meant. When he took off his underwear I wanted to see what he was working with. The room was dark so I reached for his penis. I was going to stroke it, but as I moved my hand to do it, it wasn't there. I reached for it again and when I moved my hand to stroke it, it was not there. I took two fingers and held it up so I could see what he had. It was only a peepee, not even three inches. I said to myself, "I'll be damn". Now I knew what he meant. I did not want to hurt his feelings so I didn't say anything. I was very very disappointed. Thru the whole ordeal of having sex I was faking it (I remembered the first time I had to fake it). I said if I keep this up I will be beyond frustrated. He was a nice guy but he had such a little penis. This made me wonder about everything he told me. I found out where he lived by accident. I was watching the news one day and there was a series of break ins on the street that he told me he lived on. I told him about the news report, but he said he had not seen it and none of his neighbors told him anything about any robberies. I thought that was strange. He had given me his address, so one day me and one of my girlfriends went to look for his house. The address he gave me didn't exist. I didn't mention a thing to him. I asked him more about his job. He told me he took care of Head Injury Patients. He said he would take them on field trips in their company van. One night me and my girlfriend found out where he claimed he worked and we went to investigate. I spotted his car in the parking lot. We looked in the car and it looked like someone was actually living in the car. There was food everywhere, clothes and shoes in the front and back seat, towels and paper everywhere. I was shocked. I saw clothes that I had seen him wear. I said I was dating a homeless man. He lied to me and I didn't want anymore to do with him. I never told him I knew the truth. He made the break up easy because he disappeared for about three weeks. I wondered if he saw me looking in his car that night. When I finally heard from him I told him there was no need for him to come by because I did not want to see him anymore. I told him when he decided to take off and not call me, I decided he couldn't possibly care anything about me. He told me he felt like I was smothering him and he needed to get away. I didn't ask him to explain, I knew he saw me that night. He forgot I still had a bag full of his jewelry. I took the bag to work and I had a Going Out of Business Sale. I sold the watches for $5.00, the earrings for $1.00, and the necklace sets for $2.00. I sold out in two days. I made about $200. I managed to get a little something after all. I couldn't get an orgasm, but I got money instead. Oh, I almost forgot to mention the job he claimed he had, turn out that he was the janitor at the nursing home.

Chapter 32

I went to my High School Grand Class Reunion. It was for the classes of 1964-1995. I saw a lot of my schoolmates and schoolmates of my bothers and sister. It was an amazing night. I took one of my girlfriends with me and she even saw someone she knew. I was having a ball. Then one of my schoolmates walked in the door and for some reason I could not take my eyes off him. That was strange because we never dated in high school and I never saw him until that night. He made his way around the room speaking and talking to people. When he got to me he stopped. We looked each other up and down and then we hugged. I told him it was good to see him and he said it was good to see me. He said I looked amazing. I told him he looked good too. He asked if I came with anyone and I said only with a girlfriend.

I saw him come in by himself. As we were talking some other people spotted him and came over to him and starting talking to him. He told me not to leave without giving him my telephone number. I said okay. The other people took him away. While he was talking to other people I could see him looking at me. I looked at him and smiled. After all these years of not dating any one that I went to high school with, there was a chance that was about to change. He somehow made his way back to me and he asked for my telephone number. He said he wanted to talk to me again but not at the reunion. I told him that would be nice. I gave him my telephone number and I left shortly afterwards. The reunion was on a Sunday. He called me on Wednesday. He wanted to come over on Saturday. When he came over he brought his neice with him. We sat down in the living room to talk and he asked me if his neice could go in another room and watch a movie. I took her to my TV room and gave her the remote and she was okay with that. I went back to the living room. This was John #25. We talked about our high school days.

He told me he had a crush on me in high school, but he was too scared to talk to me. I laughed. We talked about the years after high school. I told him I had been married twice and divorced twice. He told me he was married, but his wife has left him again and this time she has asked for a divorce. We both didn't have any children. The son he had died, but he did not want to go into detail, so I did not ask. We decided we would see each other. We talked for a couple of hours and then he said he had to leave. I went to get his neice and she had fallen asleep watching the movie.

She went out the door ahead of him to get in the car. He gave me a long and passionate kiss and he said it is a good thing he had to go. I laughed and closed the door. He called me the next day and said he would like to see me again. I asked him if he would like to go on a picnic. He said that would be nice. I was planning an indoor picnic. He was coming that weekend, this time by himself. I had time to buy everything we would need for our picnic.

I already had a Picnic Basket. For our picnic I had Fried Chicken, Barbeque Ribs, Potato Salad, Baked Beans, Ice Tea (everything was store bought).

I figured for dessert we could go out. The day for the picnic came. I spread a blanket on the floor in my TV room. I put on my CDs with all the old Motown songs. I placed flowers all around the blanket and I opened the blinds so the sun could shine in, and I opened my balcony door so we could hear the birds sing. I was ready for him, so I closed the door to the TV room. When he got there he thought we were going to a park for our picnic. I told him I just had to go and put on my shoes and I would be ready. He sat down and waited for me. I came back to the living room and asked him if he was ready for the picnic. He said yes. I said before we go let me show you some thing. He followed me to the TV room. I opened the door and said we just walked to our picnic spot. He said "Wow, you did all this for me?" We sat down on the blanket and he gave me a kiss. Everything was laid out, so I told him to help himself. He fixed his plate and I fixed my plate. We ate and enjoyed the music and conversation. I pulled out our yearbook. He didn't know what to say. We flashed back on memories. He gave me another kiss, this one was longer and much more passionate. Things started heating up, but I pulled back. There was no sex that day, but I knew that both of us really wanted to do it. There was no going out for dessert, we both agreed to end the date. For our next date we went to the movies and then we went out to eat. We went back to my apartment and we could not stop what happened next.

We had sex and it was good. John #25 just stared at me when it was over, because he couldn't believe he had done something he had wanted to do when we were in high school. I was his Dream girl. We continued to date and I even went out of town with him to watch his neice play in a Basketball Tournament. It was for four days. I really enjoyed watching the girls play. I met some of his friend that lived in the city where the tournament was held. I was really starting to like him until one day when I got a phone call. It was his wife.

She was furious that I was messing around with her husband. I was furious when I saw that the number she was calling me from was his phone and I heard him in the background. We had a heated exchange of words. I found out she had not left him and she was not divorcing him. He even had the nerve to call me the next day and I told him because he lied to me not to call me anymore. The next year at our Grand Class Reunion he was there and he told me he missed me. I told him to tell it to his wife and I walked away. When I got home I got on my computer and went on Facebook and did another search for Jerome. I didn't find him. I really wanted to see him again.

Chapter 33

A few months went by and one day at work one of my co-workers told me she had Thanksgiving Dinner at her house, and her husbands brother, nephew and friend had asked her when was she going to introduce them to some of her co-workers. She said she thought of me and two other co-workers. She said she tried calling us, but none of us answered our phones. She said she told them she would talk to us and try to set something up. She told me about the guy she wanted me to meet. He was five years younger than me, which was alright with me. He had never been married, but he had a daughter and a granddaughter. She told me where he worked and he had his own house and car. I said I wouldn't mind meeting him. She asked me if it would be okay for her to give him my telephone number or would I like to have his number. I told her I want him to be the first to call, so she can give him my number. He called me within a couple of hours. I went into a conference room to talk to him. We talked for about an hour. He told me somethings about himself and he said he wished he had met me sooner. I thought that was a strange remark, and I figured he was about to share some breaking news with me. He said he was seeing someone else, but he would like to be friends with me. I told him you can never have too many friends. I thanked him for being honest with me. He said he called because he was curious about how my voice would sound. I told him he had a nice speaking voice as well. We agreed we would talk again, and I hung up and went back to work. I guess hearing my voice was not enough for him, because he called me two days later and asked if he could come by so we could officially meet face to face. I told him that would be fine. He came by after he got off work that day. We were the same height, he was bald with a stocky body. I said to myself he was a sexy man. He told me I was a beautiful woman, which he could tell from my voice. We talked for a while and then he left. He continued calling me and coming over. I wondered about his relationship with the other woman, but I never mentioned it. He was John #26. One night when he came over after work I knew things were about to change. When he came in he gave me a kiss. It was so good, I gave him one. We kissed our way to the bedroom and we had some fantastic sex. He did some things and I did some things, and we both were very well pleased. Not too long after that night I found out the woman he was seeing and living with moved out. We continued seeing each other and having fantastic sex. We went out to dinner a few times. I met his mother, daughter and granddaughter when I attended a wedding that he was in (I knew the groom). I felt a little guilty about his breakup with the other woman, but then my selfish side wanted to keep having that good sex. This went on for months. I don't know why I thought he would be with only me, because he was with someone else when he met me. I found out another woman had moved in with him. He didn't know how I found out, but my friend that introduced us told me. I wasn't sure how I felt about it, but he kept calling and coming over. The more and more I thought about it, the more it seemed to bother me. He told me he had a vacation week coming up and I thought he was going to spend it with me. He went out of town with the woman he was living with and he called me everyday. I felt like a Mistress, and I didn't like it. He would send me pictures of himself with no clothes on. I couldn't get excited because he was out of town with another woman. I told him to stop sending me pictures and I deleted them from my phone. This relationship faded out because I got tired of being the other woman. If it were up to him, he would have kept things going just the way they were, because he was having his cake and eating it too. My co-worker seemed surprised we didn't work out, but how could we. He had another woman. I thought about Jerome and how I knew he only had eyes for me. I got on my computer and searched for him on Facebook again. No luck. I found out about other ways to search for people. I tried a couple of other sites. No luck.

Chapter 34

Several months went by and my co-worker was on her cell phone at work talking to one of her cousins. When she saw me coming down the hall I heard her tell the person she was talking to that she had the perfect person for him to meet. When she hung up the phone, once again, she approached me to tell me about that man. She told me he was a nice church going man, as a matter of fact she said he had been called into the ministry. She told me he is divorced, he has one son, he works and he has his own house and car. She said he had been trying to find the right woman but he has not had any luck, and she think we would be good together. She said we both love the church. I told her he sounds like a good guy, but the last guy she introduced me to did not work out. I didn't know if I wanted to try again. I told her to let me think about it for a couple of days. A couple of days later she asked me if I would like to meet him. I told her I guess it wouldn't hurt to meet him. She called him and gave him my number. He called me that evening. We talked for a couple of hours. The weekend was coming up and we wanted to see each other. He was John #27. He came over on Friday after I got off work. He worked the night shift at his job. We were laughing and talking and the next thing I knew we were having sex on the couch. I don't remember how it happened, but it did. We both were out of breath and realized it should not have happened. He was so angry with himself for letting it happen. We cleaned up and got dressed and he left. He called me the next day and apologized to me. I told him I felt bad too. He said he would have to talk to his pastor, because that behavior was not proper for a Man of God. He told me I would not hear from him until he has had a chance to talk with his pastor. I realized this was a serious matter. It was a week before he called me. He told me he had a long talk with his pastor, and he told his pastor everything that happened. He told him that he really liked me, and he was very attracted to me. His pastor told him he either had to stop seeing me or he had to be strong and not let this happen again. He did not want to stop seeing me. He told me we could not have sex anymore if we continue to see each other. He asked me if I could handle that. He said the next time he have sex he wanted it to be with his wife. I told him I knew how important it was for him being a new minister to do things decently and in order. I told him I could handle it. I invited him over for dinner the following Sunday. We ate and went into the TV room to watch a movie. Dinner was so good that he laid down on the couch to watch the movie. I sat on the other end. Everything was going good. I noticed that he was drifting off to sleep, so I shook him to wake him up so he wouldn't miss the movie. He opened his eyes and started watching the movie. He was drifting off again. This time I leaned over to whisper in his ear and give him a kiss and he woke up and grabbed me. He gave me a passionate kiss and we had some very passionate sex. We did it over and over again. It was obvious we could not resist each other. He said he didn't know what to do. We cleaned up and got dressed. He gave me a long and very passionate kiss and he left. Weeks had gone by and I had not heard from him. I went to his church one Sunday and he was there. When he saw me he smiled. After service he came up to me and told me he was glad to see me and he wanted to talk to me later. He said he would call me that evening. He called me that night from work. He asked me to come to his job so we could talk. I went to his job to hear what he had to say. He told me we had to stop having sex because it was really affecting his studies. As much as he liked me, he said he has accepted his calling into the ministry, and that requires him to live a holy life style. He said he should only be having sex with his wife. He said if I am the one, we should be able to wait until we are married. I told him it is going to take effort from both of us. His lunch break was coming up and he wanted to go back to my apartment and show me that he could be strong, because a lot was at stake. I told him he did not need to prove anything to me, just be honest with himself. He insisted he had to do this. So we went to my apartment. His job was only ten minutes away. We sat down to talk, but he wanted to sit close. I told him I thought this was a bad idea. We continued to talk. He was looking in my eyes and I was looking in his eyes. At that moment I realized he wasn't there to prove a point, he was there to have sex. I should have realized he was letting me know that I was not the one for him. Not another word was said. We were butt naked and we headed for the bed. If we were going to be strong we had time to stop. We fell on the bed in a hot embrace and needless to say, his lunch break lasted over an hour. We both knew that would be the last time we saw each other, because we could not keep our hands off each other. He gave me a long and hot steamy kiss before we left out the door, and I took him back to his job and I immediately went back home. I asked myself what was I doing. This was not me. He was not the first preacher I had dated. I knew what was expected of him. Why was I acting like a sex craved woman. I was missing something. I wasn't feeling something. I could not figure out what it was. I got back on my computer and I tried a couple other sites still trying to find Jerome. I just wanted to know where he was. Still no luck.

Chapter 35

It was 2012 and I was about to make the biggest mistake of my life. This same co-worker just kept insisting that she could find the right man for me. I should have put a stop to it, but I didn't. I wanted to see who she had picked out for me this time. I should have known this was not going to be good when she said there is something I needed to know about him first. She said she didn't know how I would take it. I should have told her not to go any further, but I didn't. She said he was in prison. I looked at her and threw up my hands. She said he is a good guy, he just got caught up in something with his friends. She said he needs the right kind of woman to help him go straight, and she thought that I could be that woman. I said to myself, what the hell, maybe someone locked up will appreciate me more. I asked her what was his crime. She said he was selling drugs. She said since he had been locked up he said he would never sell drugs again. I asked her how long had he been in prison. He had already done 10 years, and his sentence was 12 years. My gut told me to pass on this one, but I didn't follow my gut. I told her I would write him a letter and see what kind of response I got. I wrote the letter and he sent me a three page response. He was ten years younger than me. He had very nice handwriting and in his letter he sounded happy to meet me. Of course he was happy to get a letter, he was in prison. He was John #28. I wrote him every week and he answered every week. He asked for a picture of me, so I sent him the picture of me that I had on my book cover. He sent me a picture of him that he took when his daughters came to see him. He had six kids. They lived with him until he went to prison. He never married their mother. My birthday was coming up and I told him I was coming to see him. There were forms that I had to fill out before I was allowed to visit him. My forms were approved and I was put on the visitor list. I was also approved for him to be able to call me and send me emails. I couldn't believe I was actually going to prison to visit someone I had just met. I didn't tell any of my close friends about him. I planned to spend the whole weekend visiting him. The weekend that I picked came and my co-worker and her husband made the trip with me. John #28 was a friend of her husband. When he saw me he just said, "Wow". We were allowed to have one kiss when I got there and one kiss when I was leaving. I spent the entire day with him Friday, Saturday and half the day on Sunday. I enjoyed my time with him. I wasn't thinking clearly because I should have known he would be charming and sweet because he was in prison and he wanted me to keep writing him and putting money in his account. Yes I was sending him money every payday. We continued to write and his letters were full of promises of things we would do once he got home. I fell for it all like a rock. He came home early, the beginning of next year. He had to stay in a Half Way House for the first six months. I should have known better, as soon as he got home he wanted to see his friends more than he wanted to see me. I thought a man that had been away for so long would want to spend everyday with his woman making love to her. Not this man. It was several days before we even had sex and it was only okay. He spent all of his time with his friends and we never did any of the things that he wrote about in his letters. He would spend time with me when he needed something. I should have walked away from this. I think we had sex one more time before he got sent back to prison for breaking the rules at the Half Way House. He got caught smoking weed with his friends. He felt so ashamed and stupid because he had let down everyone that cared about him, and there was nothing he could say on his behalf. He messed up. He had to go back and finish out the rest of his original sentence. That meant he would get out in the beginning of the following year. I stopped writing him and accepting his calls after I got a disturbing email from one of his prison buddies, and I didn't give him permission to give my email to anyone else. His buddy implied that they had a special kind of relationship, and I didn't know how to interpret that. So I asked my co-workers husband, who was his friend, and he said it sounds like he is his girlfriend. I was mad at myself for wasting all this time on that guy. It was clear when he got home that I was only someone to write to and send him money. Everything he promised in his letters were lies. February came and he was home, but I didn't hear from him. There was talk going around about him and the guy in prison. I didn't start the rumor. It was started by his friends, but he would never admit they started the rumor. He wanted to blame me. I was having Foot Surgery in March and I wanted to have some closure to our relation ship, so I contacted his mother and told her I needed to talk to John #28. She gave me his cell phone number and told me to call him. I called him and I could hear in his voice how happy he was to hear from me. I thought it was happy, maybe it was something else. We decided to meet so we could talk things out. I settled the issue about the rumor, and told him only his friends could have spread that rumor because I didn't know his friends or his relatives. He still wouldn't admit they did it. The light bulb in my head should have went on. We were friends again, but it wasn't what I expected. I tried to help him stand on his own and not rely on his friends. I tried to help him get things for himself and not depend on them to get things for him. I was still fighting a losing battle when it came to me verse his friends. I should have cut my losses and went on my way. But not me, I was always trying to help someone do better. I should have realized everybody don't want to do better. This time it cost me a whole lot more than I bargained for. I helped him get a car. This was a major mistake. He never came to see me and I very seldom saw him. There were also other women, but he thought he was so slick that I didn't know. I just didn't speak about everything I knew. I had been around the block a few times and I wasn't blind or stupid. John #28 was a big user, and I let him use me. I knew better. He didn't realize I was only trying to help him live a better life. Stupid man. In the end I wound up taking the car and turning it in. I learned my lesson the very expensive way. I didn't see or hear from him anymore. I went back on Facebook and tried to find Jerome. I found a Jerome Adams, but when I clicked on the picture to see if it was him, it wasn't. I hit the wrong button by mistake and sent that guy a Friend Request. That guy accepted the request and he stayed on my Friend List for about two years and then he dropped off. I still hadn't found the right Jerome. Everytime I put in his name I would get a different group. I tried looking for him in Missing Persons, Criminal Files and his high school website. I didn't know his birthdate or the year he graduated, so I just guessed. I still did not find him.

Chapter 36

It was October 2013 and one of my co-workers was going to retire. Her last day was at the end of the month. All the plans had been made. We were going to take her out to lunch and come back and have a short program for her with all of her family and friends present. My co-worker had asked me to sing at her program and I agreed. We had a really good time at lunch, some of her family was there. We came back to the building for her program. Different people got up to give their comments about their relationship with her. Her brother was there and he told some real funny stories about her. After everyone had a chance to speak it was time for my song. The song she had chosen was "At Last". I tailored it to fit the occassion. She was very pleased when I finished. She gave her final remarks and we moved on to the cake and punch social. I was helping with the serving of the cake and punch. While I was standing at the table setting things up her brother walked over to me and struck up a conversation. He was a very handsome man. We talked for about ten minutes, then he went to talk to his sister. Everyone had a good time. A couple days later my co-worker called me at home and told me her brother had asked her to call me and give me his telephone number, because he wanted me to call him so we could talk. She gave me his number and I called him. He was John #29. We talked for almost an hour. He said he would like to get better acquainted with me. We both shared information about ourselves. He called me daily while he was at work. We talked for a week and he asked to take me out. We went out to dinner at an Italian Restaurant. The food was great and the conversation too. After dinner we went back to his place. We talked for a short while and I said I had to go. I had driven my car to his place and we rode in his car to the restaurant. He walked me out to my car and he gave me a sweet kiss. It was a pleasant evening. He continued to call me daily. He told me he had a day off coming up and we agreed to spend the day together. I took that day off too. I drove to his place. We watched some movies. I guess he decided it was time for him to make a move. He put his arms around me and pulled me toward him for a kiss. This time it was a tongue thrashing kiss. I felt his hands moving across my back and heading toward my breast. He pulled me down on the sofa and it was obvious what he wanted. He got up and took me by the hand and led me to his bedroom. We both started undressing. He sat on the bed to put on a condom and then he got on top of me. He had a hard time finding my hole and penetrating me, and it only lasted a very few minutes when he did. I was disappointed, but I didn't let it show. After we cleaned up and put our clother back on, we were both hungry. We ordered out and I went to pick up our food, but he paid for it. I went because after the disappointment in the bedroom I needed some fresh air. I also thought about just leaving and not coming back, but I didn't want to seem rude. When I got back he received a phone call. He had to leave shortly, so after we finished eating, I left. This time there was no good bye kiss. I felt like I wasted a day off work for nothing. I thought getting with him was going to be thrilling. It wasn't. Two days later I received a text message from him saying he did not think we should continue seeing each other, because he had some unresolved issues with his former girlfriend. I was hurt and angry that he wasn't man enough to at least call me and tell me, instead of acting like a little boy and send me a text message. That was the last time I heard from him. I said it was no great loss.

Chapter 37

It was the end of December when one of my co-workers daughter said she had the perfect guy for me. I guess everyone thought I needed to be with someone, so they were trying to help. She said he was a hard working nice man and very handsome. She worked with him. She called me from her phone and introduced us. We talked for a few minutes and he asked me to come down to where they worked so we could see each other face to face. I told him I would come when I got off work. I went to meet him, and she was right, he was very handsome. He told me I was a beautiful woman and he was glad we had been introduced. We exchanged telephone numbers. He was John #30. We talked for a week and he told me his birthday was coming up in January. I told him I would like to spend his birthday with him. He agreed. I gave him a small birthday present as a token of friendship (a tie pin) and he was surprised I gave him anything. I took him to a fine Italian Restaurant for dinner. The atmosphere was perfect for a romantic dinner. He was very impressed. I told the waiter it was his birthday and they brought him a special dessert. He was so happy. After dinner we went back to his house. I found out he lived with his mother. I thought maybe she was ill and needed someone to be with her. While I was there his mother came home from the Casino. She was not old and sickly. We talked for a while and then I left. He walked me to my car and gave me a nice kiss. I didn't hear from him for several days. I just happened to go out on Facebook and I saw pictures of him with another woman with a caption that said, he spent his birthday with a very special woman in his life. Then I got a call from my co-workers daughter telling me to stop seeing that man because they found out at their job that he is a crack addict. I was so shocked. I guess I wasn't looking for anything like that when I met him, because I had learned a lot about crack from my ex-husband. I didn't notice any signs. I knew I did not want to go back down that road again. I asked her if they were sure. She told me someone at work caught him in the act and he was fired. A few days later John #30 mother called me and she was frantic. She said he had been arrested and she needed to get him an attorney. She asked me if I could help her. The first thing I thought of was this sounds like a scam or a shake down. I told her I didn't have any attorney information and I didn't have any money that I could give her. I told her if I came up with anything I would call her. He called me a few days later and said it was all just a case of mistaken identity. After that he just faded away from me. I started seeing more pictures of him and that other woman on Facebook. I felt relieved and I didn't miss him. I told all of my friends and co-workers to stop trying to find the perfect guy for me. I told them to not introduce me to anyone else. I told them I was fine by myself. I said if the Lord wants me to have someone, He will send him. Until that time, I am good.

Chapter 38

It was 2014 and this was the year I was planning to retire. I thought about all the ups and downs that I had experienced, but God brought me through it all. I thought about all the men that had come and gone in my life. Some of them came back again. John #1 came back ten years later from the time we met. We tried to get back together. I ran into him at the mall and we went to a concert together. After the concert we went out to eat and then back to my apartment. During the concert I was trying to remember why I broke up with him. At dinner I remembered, it was because he was so boring to me. He still was. I tried to be pleasant and thought maybe I wasn't giving him a fair chance. We were older and maybe I just needed to really pay close attention to him and see what he is all about. I listened to his conversation and asked him what had he done since we last saw each other. I remember he told me he had served in the Army, after that I don't remember what else he said. But I do remember him trying hard to rekindle the flame. We had sex that night. I did it because I said to myself he had waited all these years for this moment and I was going to let him have it. He took his time and he was very gentle. It was good and very passionate, but it didn't make my toes curl. Afterwards we talked and I realized he was still boring to me. I never saw him again after that night. John #7 came back about five years after we met. I was out but I don't remember where, and I ran into him. We hooked up and went to a wedding together. He still liked me and we had a good time at the wedding. When we got back to my apartment I was trying to remember what went wrong with us. I remembered he was a student and we shouldn't have been together at that time. Then I tried to remember what was the other reason. It came back to me when we ended up in bed. The sex was the same, unfulfilling. I think this time he knew I was not pleased with his performance. We drifted apart again. John #18 came back a couple of times. When we got together we always ended up arguing. He was still very opinionated and he still thought he knew everything and I knew nothing. The last time we got together I ended up cussing him out. I was totally thru with him this time. John #26 came back several times too. We met strictly to have sex. Sex with him was very good, but I noticed that he was starting to get aggressive. I sometimes felt like he was too aggressive. He made me feel like he was taking sex from me whether I wanted it or not. I started feeling uneasy with him. I wondered if his behavior had anything to do with the women in his life moving out of his house by choice. I didn't like the way he was making me feel, so I stopped seeing him about three years ago. I realize you can't always go back. So I stopped looking back and look toward the future. There was a lot I needed to do if I wanted to retire that year. I needed to get some kind of order in my life. I promised myself after I retired that if I had not found Jerome I was going to search for him full time. Of all the men I had been with, he was the only one that I really wanted to see again. I remember the fun we had together and how we enjoyed talking to each other. He was always so kind and caring with me. My family liked him because they could tell that he really liked me. My mother liked him because he was always respectful to her. I missed him and I wanted to find him. I found six other websites I could use to look for him. My search had gotten serious. What a variety of men I had had in my life. All those relationships and none of them worked. I was beginning to wonder was there something wrong with me. I say that I am looking for something, but I don't know what it is. I say I should feel something, but I can't describe the feeling. All I knew was when I was with Jerome he made me feel like no one else ever had, and it was a very good feeling. I wanted that feeling back. I retired on the same date that I was hired into the company thirty years ago, on November 26. It was a day no one at Blue Cross or me will ever forget. I arrived to work in a stretch Limosine, and when I got out of the car I had on a Black and Gold Formal Gown with a train. My co-workers had laid out special floor covering for me to walk on. I had requested Red Carpet. There was a group of people taking pictures of me as I stepped out of the Limo. I felt like a movie star. I spent the whole day walking around saying my good byes to everyone. We went to lunch and I was the center of attention as I strolled to the restaurant. It was my day. There was a program for me in the auditorium and I made my grand entrance. Numerous people gave their remarks about me, and they almost made me speechless. Almost! I made my speech and told a few jokes and then I sang my farewell song, "It's Time To Go Now". My superviser had the companys photographer take pictures. I really enjoyed my day, but in the back of my mind I would have liked to shared it with someone special (Jerome). I got into the Limosine and went home. It was the day before Thanksgiving and I was having dinner at my apartment for my family. I was cooking most of the meal. I had a lot to be thankful for.

Chapter 39

It was the middle of 2015 and there was no one in my life. I just wanted to be by myself. I was tired of being lied to, being cheated on, being taken for granted, being someones option and not their priority, going from one guy to another. I was tired of dating. I continued searching for Jerome. I had decided if I ever see him again and get the chance to talk to him, there was something I wanted to say to him. I didn't care if he was married or living with someone. I said if I got the chance I was going to walk up to him and whisper in his ear these words, "We have some unfinished business". Then I would turn around and slowly walk away. He would know what I meant. There was never any closure for us, we just went our separate ways. We didn't break up or have any kind of falling out. We didn't even argue. One minute we were together, and then we weren't. My feelings for him didn't stop either, they kept going. He is still in my heart and mind and I can't forget him. Seeing him again will either put an end to these feelings or increase them. I want to see if he can make me feel like he did when we first met. No one else came close. We may have out grown each other and there is nothing there anymore. I just want to see him so this matter can be settled. I stopped dating so I decided I would keep myself busy doing the things I said I would do when I retired. I said I would do many things with my church. I worked on many projects with my Pastor. I had a few projects of my own, like feeding families for Thanksgiving. I fed five families each year until my money ran out. There was a lot of things to do. Someone always needed help from the church. Every year for our Annual Church Picnic I would provide all the games and prizes. I loved doing that. I was keeping busy. In September my Pastor and a group of us from church went to Florida. We went to see the Holy Land Experience Exhibit. We rented a fifteen seat passenger van and I drove all the way there (16 hours). It was amazing. We stayed a week, and I drove all the way back (19 hours). I knew I could drive long distance, but I surprised myself. Time went by and it was 2016. My finances were starting to change. There was a lot of things that I had to give up. I couldn't get my hair or nails done every other week. I couldn't go out to eat whenever I wanted. I couldn't go shopping anymore. I couldn't afford the payments for my car, so I had to turn it in. I thought things would be alright since I made all those conssessions, but I was wrong. I still had to make payments for my car, because when the finance company auctioned the car off they didn't get the full amount of what was owed on the car. I was still responsible for the remaining balance. Things may not be going the way I imagined, but thru it all God is keeping me. I count everyday a blessing, and everday God shows His love for me when he wakes me up. I thought about a movie called Mahogonay, starring Diana Ross and Billy Dee Williams. In the movie Billy Dee told Diana Ross that success is nothing if you don't have someone to share it with. I always remember that line, and I find it to be true. I think about all the successes in my life and I've only really enjoyed them when I had someone to share them with. My High School Graduation I shared with my family. My College Graduation I shared with my family and boyfriend. My first job a a Teacher I shared with my family. My first marriage I shared with a man I thought loved me. My second marriage I shared with a man I thought I would be with forever. But when it came to my Retirement I came home by myself. There was no one to meet me at the door and tell me how happy they were for me. No one to share my days of leisure. Retirement is a big step. I would love to have someone to share my retirement years and grow old together. I would love to wake up every morning in his arms. This made me take a long look at myself. What kind of person am I? Can I explain me? I have to thank God and my mother for the kind of person that I am. Sometimes even I don't understand myself. All my life I have always wanted to help somebody. God gave me a giving spirit and I know my ministry is in helping. My mother always told me to do my best in everything that I do. When it comes to helping people that I care about I want to give them the best of me. I want my best to help them to be their best. I do things for people out of my heart and I want that to show in everything that I do. Most of the time my help is misused and abused. People think they are using me or getting over on me. But they don't realize that I do what I do because I genuinely care. I don't do things looking for anything in return. I want the people around me to live their best life, and if I can help them to do that, that is what I will do. In all my relationships I gave my best. I never want anyone to say that I didn't care or really love them. My actions will always speak loudly.

Chapter 40

Time kept moving. The year of 2017 was just a year of me keeping busy and working thru the church. There were no new love connections or old flames returning. It was a whole year of me. Time waits for no one. It was April of 2018 and I had not idea that my life was about to be impacted forever. I will never forget that day, April 17. I got up that morning as usual and didn't really have any special plans for the day. I ate breakfast and then I sat down to watch my morning programs that I normally watch. I decided to get out my laptop and see what was going on on Facebook. I decided I would try again to find Jerome, but this time I told myself and the Lord this would be the last time I search for him. I said I was tired of getting disappointed when I couldn't find him. I said if I don't find him this time, it was not meant for me to find him and I would give up. I put his name in the search, Jerome Adams. I got another new group of Jeromes. Several of them had a picture, but one of them was white. I clicked on one of the black men, but it clearly wasn't him. The guy was too young. I clicked on the other picture. When it came up I stared at it for a minute. I clicked on it to make the picture bigger. I looked at that picture for about 5 minutes. I said to myself, I know this is him. I looked at the eyes, nose and mouth and I felt my heart start beating fast. I immediately sent a friend request to see if the guy would answer. The request came back in a matter of seconds saying the guy accepted my request. I started getting excited. Then I thought about all the other attempts and I decided I would ask him a question to see what his answer would be. I typed in a question. I asked him if he was the Jerome who drove the bus for DOT in Detroit.

His response came back immediately. He said yes. I hollered, "It's him, it's him". Before I could type in another question he was calling me on Facebook. I didn't know you could call on Facebook, so I didn't know how to answer the call. The call stopped ringing. I was frantic. Then it started ringing again. This time I typed in a message to him asking him how do I answer the call. The call stopped ringing again as I was waiting for him to reply to my message. I was totally flustered. Then it rang again and this time I noticed on the screen it told me what to do. I clicked on the call and I heard him say, "Hello". I felt like that 17 year old girl at the club. I said, "Is it really you?" He said, "Yes Baby, it's me." I felt a tingle go thru me when I heard his voice. I felt something that I could not explain. We talked for about an hour. It was like we had been talking all the time. This felt good and there was no laspe in our conversation. I thought about the statement that I said I was going to say to him if I ever got the chance to talk to him. I was getting ready to say it, but he said the exact same statement to me. He said, "We got some unfinished business". I hollered and said, "What did you say to me?" He said it again. I laughed and told him I couldn't believe what he had just said to me. He said, "But it's true." I told him that I was just getting ready to say the exact same thing to him, but he beat me to it. We both laughed. We both knew at that moment that we were Soulmates. He told me this was his first time on Facebook and he only went on it that day because he wanted to see what was on it. He said when he got my friend request and saw my picture, he wasn't sure, but he responded right away. But when I asked him the question about driving the bus for DOT, he knew it had to be someone from his past that knew him. He said he had to call and see who this person was. He said when he heard my voice he knew it was me. He said he had been praying that he would see me again. He said he never forgot me and he had been trying to find someone that made him feel like I did when we met. I told him I had been looking for someone that could make me feel like I felt with him the night we met. I told him I never could find anyone that gave me that feeling. We talked about the night we met. He remembered what I was wearing that night and he remembered the song that was playing when he asked me to dance. I remembered what he said to me when we got on the dance floor. I remembered it was a slow song and he whispered in my ear. Between the two of us we relived that night. We talked about a lot of things that happened when we started dating. We talked about our lives after we went our separate ways. Our conversation just flowed like we had never stopped seeing each other. It felt so good talking to him. It felt so right. We agreed we needed to see each other face to face so we could see if the feelings were still there. But from our conversation on the phone, we already knew how we felt about each other. We both said we knew that God had brought us back together. We both had asked God to let us see each other again. God allowed it to happen in His own time. We both were thankful to God that He loved us so much that He allowed our love to stand strong thru the test of time.

Chapter 41

It was the day that I had been waiting for. Jerome was coming over and I would be standing face to face with the love of my life. I would be looking into the eyes of the man that fell in love with me the moment he saw me. The man who won my heart after he asked me to dance. The man who never forgot me. The man I often thought about thru the years. The man who made me feel things no one else ever could. The man that I knew truly loved me for me. The man I tried to find in every man I met. The man who has loved me for over 40 years. He was on his way. I can't describe how I felt, my feelings were all over the place. I wasn't nervous, I was excited. I felt that 17 year old girl rise up in me. I tried on numerous outfits trying to pick the right one to have on, so when I opened the door his mouth would fall open and he would be speechless. I finally decided on an outfit. I would wear a skirt and sleeveless top with sandals that matched my top. I coordinated all my jewelry to match my top. I covered my whole body with some Apple Blossom and Lavendar Lotion. I wished I could have gotten my hair done, but I had to work with it myself. I smoothed it all down and pulled it to the back of my head and put on a ponytail. I was ready. He had a hard time trying to get to my apartment so he had to call me and I directed him right to my door. I was looking out the window when he got out of the car. There he was, Jerome Adams. The man I had been searching for for the last ten years. The man that I fell in love with on the dance floor. I buzzed him in the entrance door, and as he walked up the stairs I stepped out into the hall. I saw his eyes light up and he had the biggest smile on his face that I had ever seen. When he came thru my door we fell into each others arms. I said, "It's really you." He said, "I have been praying for this day." I had to hold back the tears. We held each other for several minutes and then we kissed. I thought I was going to faint. I remembered his sweet kisses and they still had the same affect on me. We hugged again and kissed again. We sat down on the couch and all we could do was just look at each other and we both said we knew God had brought us back together. He told me all the feelings he had for me were still there. I told him when he walked thru the door I felt the same way I did when I left the dance floor the night we met. I told him my feelings for him had not changed. We both agreed that it felt like we had never been apart and we were just picking up from where we left off. It was an amazing reunion. We talked about the night we met and the days that we dated. He remembered a lot of things that I had forgotten, and I remembered some things that he had forgotten. We asked about old friends. All of his family had passed away, his grandmother, sister and mother. Now I understood why he was always so nice to me, he had been raised by three women. He still had that kind demeanor and I always liked that about him. I told him my mother had also passed. He asked about all of my family. It felt so comfortable talking to him. I showed him the three pictures he gave me before I left for college. He had forgotten about those pictures and he didn't remember giving them to me. I told him he gave them to me because he said he did not want me to forget him when I got to college. He was surprised I still had them. I told him I would pull them out every now and then when I thought about him. It was clear we were always on each others mind. What happened next was the only natural thing that could have happened. We made love to each other. It was amazing. I put all of my heart into every movement and I felt him do the same. We made love for over an hour. He made my toes curl and I trembled when he held me in his arms. There was no doubt in my mind he was my Soulmate. Everything felt so right. Jerome said no one ever made him feel like I do and his body still respond to me the way he used to when we were young. I remembered he would get so aroused when he pressed up against me, he would get an erection and he would have to pull His shirt out over his pants because he had to walk to the bus stop. He would have a huge wet spot on the front of his pants because he had exploded. We layed in bed in each others arms and talked about some of the things that went on in our lives. We found out we had a lot in common and we also discovered that we thought a lot alike. We were compatible in a lot of areas. I told him about the book I had written about my second marriage. He said he could relate to my story because he had a similar experience with a woman he was dating who was a Heroin Addict. We discovered we had several similar experiences. He said I needed to write a book about our reunion. He said it is like a Fairy Tale coming true and God had put it all together. I told him it sounded like a good idea, but it would take some time to write it because I would have to wait for the ending. He said the ending wouldn't be hard to write because I am never going to get away from him again. He said I should have been his wife a long time ago. I told him it wasn't our time then, but now God says it is. We talked about our past and made plans about our future. I told him I didn't want him to ever let me go. He said he had no intentions of that ever happening. He said he is in my life for the rest of my life. I liked the sound of that. I told him he is the only one that I wanted to share my retirement years. He asked me to marry him and I said I would marry him in a heartbeat. I was finally going to be with the love of my life, the man of my dreams. I thought this only happened on television or to other people, not me. But it was really happening to me and all I could do was say, "Thank you Lord". He said he told his friends he is finally going to be with the woman of his dreams. I told my family I finally get to be with the man who really and truly loved me just for me, and after all these years he still do.

Chapter 42

We talked everyday. We would talk in the morning. We would talk in the afternoon when he was on his way to work. He was working security for an auto parts store. I asked him why was he still working and he said it was just for something to do. He would call me in the middle of his shift. Each time we talked it would be over an hour. His birthday was coming up in the next month and I asked him what did he usually do for his birthday. He said he didn't do anything. I told him that is about to change. I asked him if he would mind if I made plans for his birthday. He told me to go ahead. I sat down to think about what we could do. I checked online to see if there would be any plays or concerts on that day. I checked the museums to see if there were any special events. I checked the movie guides to see what movies were playing. I checked to see if there were any scenic tours we could go on. I also checked to see if I could find a horse and carriage service for my area. I wanted his day to be special and I wanted it to be an all day celebration. I asked him what kind of food he liked to eat. I had planned to take him to a really nice Italian Restaurant for dinner and then take him to a different restaurant for dessert. My plan included him starting the day off with breakfast and ending the day at dinner. I asked him if he would take the day off work for his birthday. I think I was more excited about making the plans than he was about it being his birthday. I really looked forward to getting his phone calls everyday. He told me how much he missed me when we weren't on the phone. He told me how much he loved me and how happy he was that we are back together. I could feel the love he had for me. I loved him just as much. I had started writing our story and to my amazement it was going well. I told him that in order for me to tell our story, I would have to include every thing that had happened in my life up to the time we connected on Facebook. He said he would not have a problem with it. I told him I would have to mention all the guys that I have dated and tell about both of my marriages. He said he didn't mind. I said in my mind, he is still that cool guy that never got upset or angry with me. I loved him even more. During one of our conversations we both said there was one thing we had never done, and that was to actually sleep together. It sounded strange, but we had never spent the night together and woke up in each others arms. We lived so far from each other. It was about a 45 to 60 minute drive from his house to mine. We agreed we would spend the night together. He came over on Friday. He came straight from work. I was so excited, I felt like a little girl on Christmas morning finally getting the gift I always wanted. We talked about our plans for our future together. Since we had gotten back together Jerome was planning to retire from his job and we were going to spend the rest of our life together enjoying each other. We both agreed he would move in with me since we both liked the area where I was living. Everything we talked about felt so right. He told me every time he looked at me he just couldn't believe he found me. He said he had hoped and prayed he would see me before he left this life. I told him I never thought I would be living a Fairy Tale Life, and I have to keep telling myself this is really happening. There could not have been anyone else in the whole world who was as much in love as we were. That night we made love like it was our last day on earth. There was so much passion and love, it filled the room. He gave me pleasure from head to toe and I did likewise to him. It was an awesome night. We collapsed in each others arms and he fell asleep. I couldn't come down off the clouds. I spent a couple of hours just watching him as he slept. I kept touching him to make sure I wasn't dreaming. This was the man I had been searching for all my life. This was my true Soulmate. He is really here and he wants to be with me. He wants to spend the rest of his life with me. I finally felt myself drifting off to sleep. When we woke up the next morning, all we could do was look at each other and smile. I told him he was a bed hog because he was all over the bed. He laughed. I also told him he snored very loud. He said he snored when he was really tired and he gets real tired from being on his feet all night at work. I laughed and told him I could tell he must have been really tired. He told me he would be giving his employer notice that he would be leaving at the end of the month and he would be coming home to me. I was so happy to hear that. We got up and he cleaned up and got dressed because he said he had several things he needed to take care of. He said he was getting things in order before he came to me. He said he didn't want to come to me with any problems, so everything had to be in order. I told him that was fine with me, and I could hardly wait for him to come home to me. This time there would be no one leaving anyone behind. We were going to live the life God had intended us to have. I told him no matter what comes up we would face it together. He said that is the kind of woman he has been searching for. He gave me one of his sweet kisses and he left out the door to go handle his business.

Chapter 43

I know the comparison of a Soulmate to a John seems strange and far fetched. But not really. One is forever and one is for right now. Let me explain my thoughts. A Soulmate is two spirits that merge into one. Each gives life and power to the other. Both souls function together for one purpose and that is to experience love at its fullest and true potential. When you meet your Soulmate you know immediately he is the one. There is a connection that happens instantly. At that moment that person is the center of all your attention. You begin to communicate without saying a word. Your hearts speak to each other. You respond to each other as if you have already met a long time ago. Your spirits touch and the glow from the embrace shines thru your eyes. You have just met but your souls have already merged. You have made love to each other without even touching. A Soulmate anticipates your needs and desires without speaking a word. He knows what is needed from him to make sure that you have everything that you need to live your best life. A Soulmate inspires and encourages you to be the best that you can be. You realize your coming together is not just for sex, but for much more than that. You come together to build a life together that will stand the test of time. To a Soulmate everyday is another chance to share space with the one they love and find ways to let that person know how special they are to them. A Soulmate invests his heart into the relationship to make it a strong bond that cannot be broken. A John is someone who is just looking for a temporary good time. He just wants to feel good. His interest is purely physical. Sex is what he wants. He may hang around for a while because he likes the way you do what you do. It could be weeks, months or years. There is no merging of the souls, only merging of bodies to fulfill a lust that has to be met. You may share a few laughs, stories and adventures, but there is no spiritual connection. As long as things are going to his liking he will keep coming back. He may be with you, but he is always looking for someone else that can do some things that you don't do. When things start to get rockie and he has had enough, he will leave. This relationship is not solid. A John is not looking for a life partner, he only wants a partner. He is not trying to build a life together, his life is his own. To a John everyday is just another chance to see how much enjoyment he can get out of that day. His focus is primarily on himself, making sure he gets what he needs to be happy. A John feels that his investment of time and money in the relationship entitles him to certain benefits, like sex. Sometimes we make the mistake in thinking we have found our Soulmate, when in reality we only have a John. We try to make this person be something that he is not. We listen to our flesh instead of our spirit. The spirit knows. Then there is the person that we treat like a John, because we really only want to spend a little time with him and not get too involved. In reality he is your Soulmate. But life has a way of changing the natural order of things. The Soulmate stops listening to his heart and spirit and lets his flesh take over and becomes a John instead. This is by choice. This changes everything.

Chapter 44

It has been two months and I have not seen nor heard from Jerome. He has not called or texted me. I tried calling him but he has not answered my calls or my text messages. He has just disappeared from my life with no explanation. I wrote him a letter, but there has been no response. I was worrying myself sick about him. I wondered if he was hurt or dead. I wondered if there was another woman involved. All I can do is guess because Jerome has not tried to contact me. In my mind I keep going over everything that he said to me, and I try to see if maybe I missed something that he was trying to tell me. I keep going over the night that we spent together, maybe I missed something that he said. I could not come up with anything that could explain his disappearance. I felt so hurt and disappointed. This was not the Jerome that I remembered. As I think back to the day we first met, I remember that Jerome was always so kind and attentive to me. He never lied to me and I really liked him for that. During one of our conversations I did ask Jerome if he had any hidden motive for getting back with me. I wanted to know if he intended to win me back and then leave me like he said I did to him. He told me he finally understood why I had to leave and he no longer held that against me. He said he would never hurt me because he wanted to spend the rest of his life with me. Those words kept ringing in my head. Was that a lie? Did I fall for the biggest con game ever? Has he been carrying a grudge against me for all these years and waiting for his chance to get back at me? Did he really believe God allowed us to get back together so he could have his revenge? Did he think God works like that? He told me that he was an active member at his church and he sometimes go out and preach Gods word. If he is a Man of God then he must know that God doesn't condone deception. I know the Lord knows my heart and He knows that my feelings for Jerome are real and true. I never forgot about him and he was always in my heart. When we were together I thought I could feel the love he had for me. Whatever was going on with him did not make any sense to me. Something does not fit. I kept going over all of our conversations and there was nothing that was said that could explain his disappearance. There is no one that I can call. I can't go to his job to see if he is still working. I can't even go to his house to see if he is still living there. All I can do is wait to see if he will contact me and tell me what happened. I get angry at times because I feel that we are too old to be playing games and I should not have to guess. The least he could do is tell me if he has changed his mind about us. I have been praying for him. I pray that he is alright and nothing or no one has hurt him. I pray that one day he will find the courage to contact me. I asked the Lord to touch his heart so he will have one last act of decency and call me. I only want to talk to him so I can put this behind me and move on. I cannot get him out of my head or my heart. I only want to know the truth. I feel I deserve that much. Clearly this is not the same Jerome that I remember. I know we all go thru some changes as we grow older, but I thought we kept our same character. This is so out of character for the Jerome I fell in love with. I thought about the ending for my book. The ending is not going to be like I thought it would be. My Soulmate has turned out to be someone I don't recognize. Maybe there is no soulmate for me. Once again I am tired of being lied to and deceived. If he is not my soulmate, I don't want to try again. I have had enough heart aches and disappointments. This time I am finished. I can't take another man hurting me. I gave all of me to Jerome and he walked away from me. I have nothing left to give to anyone else. The love of God is all I need, and I know He will never leave me. Life teaches us so many lessons. Some of them are painful, but necessary. How could I have been so wrong about Jerome? I trusted my gut and it told me he is the one. I was totally blind sided, because I did not see this coming. I cannot believe this is the way he wants this to end. I meant every thing I said to him and I have no regrets. Fairy Tales do come true, but they don't always end the same for everybody. The man I thought was my soulmate has rejected me and I feel so violated. I know God will get me thru this, and I will be alright. I do not want another relationship. The only relationship I want now is with God. I know God will not reject me. He promised to never leave me or forsake me. God is His word and it is impossible for Him to lie. I've had enough Johns in my life and there is no room for any more. It is true that you cannot go back to splendor in the grass. You have to deal with the present and let the past go. I thought my past and present were the same, but I was wrong. When you grow up you have to put away childhood things. I thank God for the two months that Jerome and I spent together before he disappeared. Those days were wonderful and I will never forget them. For two months I felt so loved and special. No one can take those days from me. Whatever Jerome is doing, I pray that he is happy and living his best life. As for me, I can do all things thru Christ who strengthens me. I'm holding my head up high and moving forward. To any future John, love don't live here anymore, so please don't knock on my door. I think about all of the years that I thought about him. How I wondered where he was and how he was doing. All the years that I compared every guy that I met to him, and judged them on how they treated me, as compared to how he treated me. All the years I fantasized about what it would be like when I see him again. Year after year I searched for him. He was the only guy that I knew who never lied to me. The only guy who treated me like I was the number one priority in his life. I promised myself if he was available, I would love him to death. I would spend the rest of my life making sure that everyday he knew I loved him. I couldn't wait to see him again. I prayed for a chance to be with the man that I knew would love me forever. The day we connected on Facebook I felt my prayers had been answered. I would have never in a million years believed things would turn out this way. Some days I get angry, then I get sad, then I feel depressed, then I pray. I let my guard down and I let him have my heart again and he stomped on it.

Chapter 45

I kept praying to the Lord that He would allow me to know the truth about Jerome. I still wanted to know. Being the woman that I am, I needed to try to make some sense out of all of this so I could move on. I wanted to know what happened to make him leave me without saying a word. I prayed many nights for the Lord to answer my prayer. Then one day when I went on Facebook, someone posted a message that said, "Sometime God sends an EX back into your life to see if you are still stupid". That message made me think and everything became clear to me. God did allow our paths to come back together, but I reacted without thinking. The Word tells us to be anxious for nothing, but to pray and seek God. The Lord wanted me to see Jerome as he really was, and not the guy that I fantasized him to be. The Jerome I remembered was gone, and the Jerome that I reconnected with was nothing like him. This Jerome was a liar and he did not care for me like he did when we were young. He never forgave me for leaving him. He wanted to see me again only for the purpose of getting back at me. He wanted me to fall for him again so he could walk away from me. He said he believed God brought us together, but he didn't tell me he had been carrying a grudge against me for over forty years. He told me he understood why I had to leave and he was happy for me. He said he didn't harbor any ill feelings. He was lying right to my face. As I thought about him, now I could understand his stand off behavior. When he first saw me he was reluctant to hug me. I saw it but I just thought he was nervous. I wanted so badly for our reunion to be our second chance for romance. I wanted our reunion to be like a Fairy Tale. I wanted him to fall in love with me all over again. I wanted our life together to have the happy Fairy Tale ending, we would get married and live happy ever after. I only saw what I made myself see. After the years that I thought about him, I only had good thoughts and memories. When I saw him I saw the Jerome that I met when I was 17. I was being stupid. I believed everything that he told me. He told me that he still had the same feelings for me that he had when we first met. He said he wanted to spend the rest of his life with me. He said I should have married him when we met. He said he would never let me get away from him again. He told me he had not been with anyone for two years, because he could not find anyone like me. This was all Fairy Tale criteria. I really thought he meant everything he said. I was thinking of sharing my life with him, but he was thinking of ruining my life like he thought I did to him. I let my emotions cloud my judgment. I had been praying for Jerome to contact me and tell me the truth, but that was not Gods plan. My contact came in a dream I had one night. I dreamed that I got a very disturbing call from Jerome telling me it was his turn to hurt me and I was about to get what I deserved. I woke up feeling really strange. Everything became clear to me and I thank God it was only two months that we saw each other. I'm glad I know that God loves me and He has His way of revealing the truth. I don't hold any ill feelings towards Jerome. I don't even want any revenge. I actually need to thank him for making me let go of the past and see things as they really are. I thank him for knocking the stupid out of me. If he had not done this I would be with a man who would never be faithful to me. If he is cheating on the woman that he is with now, how can I expect him to not cheat on me. In reality he cheated on her with me. I could never trust him or believe anything that he says. I thank him for leaving me and not giving me a life full of disappointments. I won't be fantasizing about him anymore. I won't be judging others because of him. I can let him go and move on.

Chapter 46

As always I may be down for a moment, but I will rise. If he thinks that he has totally stopped me from being happy, let me set the record straight. The only thing he has done is given me a dramatic ending for my book. Now I realize there were signs along the way that I ignored because I was so caught up in the excitement of seeing him again. I remember when we connected on Facebook, we talked for two months before he came to see me. That should have been my first red flag. If he was so happy to be talking to me he would have came over right away. Every time he was suppose to come over he had an excuse why he didn't make it. I believe if you got an explanation for every thing, then you must be lying about something. When he finally came over he was hesitant to hug me and I had to ask for a kiss. I expected him to grab me as soon as he walked thru the door and paste his lips on mine. I believe at that moment he was not sure if he actually wanted to be with me again, or if he just wanted to go on with his plan. I believe he was wrestling with his true feelings for me and he did not want to give into them. My gut told me there was another woman involved and he was weighing his options. He was trying to decide which woman he wanted to be with. I think when he saw how independent I was it also bothered him. I told him I didn't need him to rescue me I needed him to love me. Maybe he felt he had to knock me down a bit. The plan for our first face to face was to spend the whole day together, but when he came in and sat down he told me he could only stay for a few hours, because he had some people waiting for him and he had to go take care of some business. That should have been the second red flag. He lied to me. In several of our conversations he asked me if we got married would I ever throw him out of the bed and make him sleep on the couch. I thought that was an odd question to ask since we had just gotten back together. Then he would ask me if I would always love him no matter what. I had no idea where he was going with this question. I told him my love was real and it was consistant. This should have been my third red flag. I believe something was going on at home with him and someone else. I soon found out why he wanted to know if I would kick him out of the bed, because he snored louder than a bull in pain. I wasn't sure if I could survive all that noise, but for love sake I was willing to try. There were other flags. He never called me when he was at home and he never called me in the evenings. When I called him in the evenings his phone would always be turned off and it would go straight to his voicemail. Everytime he called me he was either out somewhere or at work. I could never reach him once he left work. I asked him why did he keep turning his phone off and he said he did it because it would charge faster when it is off. That didn't sound right to me, but I accepted it. I could never talk to him over the weekend. If I didn't talk to him before he got off work on Friday, I would not hear from him until Monday. The same thing happened with his texting, never when he was at home or in the evening. When I asked him about this, he said he lived with his cousin and he did not want him listening to his conversations. This made no sense to me, but I accepted it. I never got any text messages from him over the weekend either. I knew there was something else going on but I was so caught up, I let it go. When he disappeared he also came off of Facebook so I could no longer reach him. He cut off all sources of contact with me. Mr. Jerome was playing the oldest game in the book and I let him play. I didn't think he would play me. But if you give an old man too much leeway he will surely try to see how much he can get away with. I can't forget what happened when we made love. He had a hard time getting a full erection, but he did good with what he had, for a man of his age. I'm sure he was embarrassed about his performance and that could be one of the reasons he don't want to see me anymore. I can under stand that, because I know I missed the years that he was probably really good in bed. Forty years is a long time and things do change. But I was willing to deal with that part as well. I loved him. I am more disappointed than I am hurt because I thought I was finally going to be with the one man in my life who never lied to me and who truly loved me with sincerity. I thought I had a man who really gave a damn. What a let down. Love make you do stupid things, and I did them. He has not destroyed me. I have gone thru so much in my life, this is just another part of my journey. He has only proved my point, and that is if he's not your Soulmate he is just another John.

About the Author

Anita is a graduate of Michigan State University, with a B.A. in elementary Education. She is a former Teacher for Highland Park, MI. She worked for Blue Cross Blue Shield of Michigan for 30 years before retiring. She is an active member of her church, Greater Bethlehem Missionary Baptist Church. she serves on multiple ministries. She survived 2 abusive marriages and numerous failed relationships. Anita's faith in God is the reason that she is able to press on when things get really bad. Nothing or no one can separate her from the love of God. She believes God said it and that settles it.